ALL together NOW

for ages 4-12

D1716834

13 Sunday school lessons when you have kids of all ages in one room

LOIS KEFFER

Author of **ALL-IN-ONE SUNDAY SCHOOL**

Group

Loveland, Colorado
group.com

Group resources really work!

This Group resource incorporates our R.E.A.L. approach to ministry. It reinforces a growing friendship with Jesus, encourages long-term learning, and results in life transformation, because it's

Relational
Learner-to-learner interaction enhances learning and builds Christian friendships.

Experiential
What learners experience through discussion and action sticks with them up to 9 times longer than what they simply hear or read.

Applicable
The aim of Christian education is to equip learners to be both hearers and doers of God's Word.

Learner-based
Learners understand and retain more when the learning process takes into consideration how they learn best.

All Together Now

Volume 3 — SPRING

Copyright © 2013, Lois Keffer

Credits
Author: Lois Keffer
Editors: Christine Yount Jones, Jennifer Hooks, Lee Sparks, and Deborah Helmers
Chief Creative Officer: Joani Schultz
Cover Designer: Jeff Spencer
Interior Designer: Jean Bruns
Production Artist: Suzi Jensen
Illustrator: Matt Wood

ISBN: 978-0-7644-8234-2
Printed in the United States of America.
10 9 8 7 6 5 4 3 2   15 14 13

Table of Contents

THE LESSONS

All Together Now

Introduction

Dear Friend in Children's Ministry,

The world is greening, the joy of spring is in the air. Time to welcome you to *All Together Now, Volume 3*! This quarter we continue through the final chapters in Jesus' life on earth, from mighty miracles that had all of Jerusalem wanting to proclaim him king, through the downward path of Holy Week and its triumphant ending as we finish our journey along the way of the King. Then we'll pick right up with the 12 who changed the world—first in Jerusalem, then in Judea, Samaria, and all the parts of the earth!

We'll begin the quarter by intercepting a mysterious night visitor to Jesus and end it by barely surviving a thrilling shipwreck with the Apostle Paul. And you and your kids won't want to miss a beat in between!

When the Jewish opposition saw Jesus' lifeless body on the cross, they thought their campaign to stamp out his new way of thinking about the kingdom of God was complete. After all, he had only a few close disciples and they were running scared—hiding out in some secret room, their hopes dashed, the savior they so passionately believed in brought down by death.

But those leaders couldn't have been more wrong! Jesus wasn't defeated. In fact, the power of God was about to burst forth, carrying Jesus' message across the entire Roman Empire and eventually the world, with an energy that only the Holy Spirit could provide.

How often during our lifetimes do we live out this same story? When all seems lost, perhaps well after all seems lost, God's will comes to light with clarity and the Spirit moves with power that takes our breath away.

Today's kids need to know this truth. They need to have it reaffirmed again and again. It's in the moment when everything seems to have melted down around us that God's power wells up, the scene begins to change, and we realize that touching bottom was just part of acknowledging that we are nothing without our great and mighty God who chose us before time began to be part of his design for the work of the kingdom of heaven on earth.

Lois Keffer

Active Learning in Combined Classes

Research shows people remember most of what they do but only a small percentage of what they hear—which means kids don't do their best learning just sitting around a table talking! They need to be involved in lively activities that help bring home the truth of the lesson. Active learning involves learning through experiences—experiences that help kids understand important principles, messages, and ideas.

Active learning is a discovery process that helps children internalize the truth as it unfolds. Kids don't sit and listen as a teacher tells them what to think and believe—they find out for themselves. Teachers also learn in the process!

Each active-learning experience in this book is followed by questions that encourage kids to share their feelings about what just happened. Further discussion questions help kids interpret their feelings and decide how this truth affects their lives. The final part of each lesson challenges kids to decide what they'll do with what they've learned—how they'll apply it to their lives during the coming week.

How do kids feel about active learning? They love it! Sunday school becomes exciting, slightly unpredictable, and more relevant and life-changing than ever before. So move the table aside, gather your props, and prepare for some unique and memorable learning experiences!

Active learning works beautifully in combined classes. Whether the group is playing a game or acting out a Bible story, kids of all ages can participate on an equal level. You don't need to worry about reading levels and writing skills. Everyone gets a chance to make important contributions to class activities and discussions.

These simple classroom tips will help you get your combined class off to a smooth start:

☐ When kids form groups, aim for an equal balance of older and younger kids in each group. Encourage the older kids to act as coaches to help younger ones get in the swing of each activity.

☐ In "pair-share," everyone works with a partner. When it's time to report to the whole group, each person tells his or her partner's response. This simple technique teaches kids to listen and to cooperate with each other.

☐ If an activity calls for reading or writing, pair young nonreaders with older kids who can lend their skills. Older kids enjoy the esteem-boost that comes with acting as a mentor, and younger kids appreciate getting special attention and broadening their skills.

☐ Don't worry too much about discussion going over the heads of younger children. They'll be stimulated by what they hear the older kids saying. You may be surprised to find some of the most insightful discussion literally coming "out of the mouths of babes."

☐ Make it a point to give everyone—not just those who are academically or athletically gifted—a chance to shine. Affirm kids for their cooperative attitudes when you see them working well together and encouraging each other.

All Together Now

□ Keep in mind kids may give unexpected answers. That's okay. When kids give "wrong" answers, don't correct them. Say something like: "That's interesting. Let's look at it from another viewpoint." Then ask for ideas from other kids. If you correct their answers, most kids will soon stop offering them.

How to Get Started With All Together Now

TEACHING STAFF

When you combine Sunday school classes, teachers get a break! Teachers who would normally be teaching in your 4- to 12-year-old age groups may want to take turns. Or ask teachers to sign up for the Sundays they'll be available to teach.

LESSONS

The lessons in the *All Together Now* series are grouped by quarter—fall, winter, spring, and summer—but each lesson can also stand on its own.

PREPARATION

Each week you'll need to gather the easy-to-find supplies in the You'll Need section and photocopy the reproducible handouts. Add to that a careful read of the lesson and Scripture passages, and you're ready to go!

Quick-Grab Activities—Plan in a Can

By Cynthia Crane and Sharon Stratmoen
Reprinted by permission of Children's Ministry Magazine. © Group Publishing, Inc. All rights reserved.

It's Sunday morning and you've just finished your entire lesson. You check the clock, and although the service should be ending, you hear no music, see no parents coming down the hall. What you *do* hear is your senior pastor, still excited about the message. And then you quickly begin trying to figure out what you're going to do with a room full of kids and no lesson left.

You need a survival kit. A bucket of backup, a plan in a can. So we've created two kits you can build on your own and store in your room. When you have extra time with kids, don't sweat it—just pull out your plan in a can and get busy!

In case you're wondering, Why call it a can? Why not a box or a bin or a bucket? For those times when you're worrying whether you'll be able to keep kids' attention and bust their boredom, the name is a sweet reminder that yes, you can!

PLAN IN A CAN: Games Galore!

THE INGREDIENTS

- ☐ Faithful Faces cards (printed photos, poster board, adhesive, and a laminator or clear adhesive vinyl) held together with a rubber band
- ☐ sidewalk chalk
- ☐ Christian music CDs for kids
- ☐ black-light lamp
- ☐ 2 large happy-face images
- ☐ 2 colors of plastic clothespins (enough for 3 per child; available at dollar stores)

FAITHFUL FACES ▸▸ Kids love the Memory Game, where shuffled cards are laid out facedown in a grid and kids try to find matching cards by turning over two at a time. (If they don't get a match, they turn the cards back facedown and the next person goes. If they do get a match, they get another turn.) So why not capitalize on this fun game to model and reinforce the important faithful faces in kids' lives? Just take pictures of the kids in your class, missionaries in your church, Bible friends you've been learning about, families you're praying for, and people in your congregation. Then whip up your own version of the game.

Use photo paper or regular printer paper to print out two of each photo, and mount them on poster board. Run the poster board through a laminator or apply clear adhesive vinyl, and you've got a game worth talking about. Kids will love finding their friends. And when they get a match, throw in a little challenge by giving them an extra point if they can remember names and other details about the person on the card.

SIDEWALK CHALK OF TODAY'S TALK ▸▸ Form groups of two to six, and hand out sidewalk chalk. You can have as many or as few groups as you have sidewalks for. Have groups work together to draw one picture on concrete that says something about the day's Bible story. When parents pick up their kids, you get a huge blessing: The kids tell their parents what they learned without being prompted. As a bonus, take photos of kids and their drawings for a quick recap to start off the following week's lesson. You can even make a month-in-review bulletin board starring your kids as the teachers.

MUSIC FREEZE ▸▸ If you think an hour is a long time for you, it's like dog years to kids. They have wiggles they've got to get out. So when you have extra time, turn up the music and let kids be as goofy as they want—until the music stops. Then they have to freeze in place. Give this a twist by adding a black light. Changing your environment is a great break from the everyday, and it lets kids know that you always have a few surprises in store.

CLOTHESPIN TAG ▸▸ You can use this game to remind kids that no thief can steal our joy when we go to the Joy Source: God. Place the happy-face images on the floor at opposite ends of a play area. Form two teams, and have each team go to one happy face. Assign each team a color of clothespin. Pin three clothespins to the back of each child's clothing above the waist. The goal of the game is for each team to try to steal the other team's clothespins and drop them on their own team's happy face. Play music to signal "go." Let kids play for one minute or so, and then turn off the music to signal "stop." After a few starts and stops, end the game, declare the team with the most clothespins as the winner, and then let kids get more "joy" on their backs and play again. When you're done, remind kids that they can always find new joy with God.

PLAN IN A CAN: Craft Creations

THE INGREDIENTS

- ☐ Legos in a resealable bag
- ☐ Moon Sand sculpting sand
- ☐ PlayFoam sculpting material
- ☐ window crayons
- ☐ Window Writers
- ☐ whiteboard markers
- ☐ Magic Nuudles cornstarch building blocks
- ☐ giant chenille pipe cleaners

- ☐ Bendaroos sculpting sticks
- ☐ one-subject notebook
- ☐ colored pencils
- ☐ Glitter Putty
- ☐ construction paper
- ☐ washable markers
- ☐ SuperBalls
- ☐ Christian music CDs for kids

CREATE ▸▸ If you have time to burn as kids are arriving, try this activity. Have kids use Legos building blocks, Moon Sand sculpting sand, PlayFoam sculpting material, Window Writers, or whiteboard markers to create a symbol of something that happened during the week. Then have kids show their creations as they say: "Hi, my name is _____, and I created this _____, because last week _____."

RESPOND ▸▸ Let kids use any craft supplies from the can to create a symbol of what the day's lesson meant to them. For instance, kids can draw a picture or write how they'll apply the point to life, using the windows, a whiteboard, or paper. Or they might choose to create a symbol that reminds them of what they learned, using giant chenille pipe cleaners or Bendaroos sculpting sticks. Invite kids to share what their creations represent.

PRAY ▸▸ Create a class prayer journal with a notebook for kids to write prayer notes in. Have kids all write their names on the cover because the journal belongs to all of them. Take out the journal throughout the year. Encourage kids to take turns writing their prayers or notes using colored pencils. If kids are stumped, give them prayer prompts such as "I thank God for..." "I need help with..." and "I pray for..." Close your time with prayer, and include requests from the prayer journal.

CHILL ▸▸ Give kids Glitter Putty, SuperBalls, or simply space. Play Christian music and let kids just "chill" as they quietly listen. Use the following tactile treats to help them focus on the music. As they listen, let them squish Glitter Putty between their fingers, play with SuperBalls, or simply relax on the floor at least 5 feet away from anyone else and close their eyes.

The Night Visitor

LESSON AIM

To help kids believe that ★ *everyone who believes in Jesus will have eternal life.*

OBJECTIVES

Kids will

✓ play a game of Uggy-Buggy Tip Tag,

✓ enjoy a visit from Nicodemus as he returns from his talk with Jesus,

✓ prepare a craft featuring John 3:16,

✓ plan ways to share their John 3:16 crafts, and

✓ commit to using a listening prayer in the coming week.

BIBLE BASIS

 **John 3:1-17**

Within the first three chapters of his Gospel, John tucks in the story of Nicodemus. You're going to like Nicodemus despite the fact that he was a Pharisee, a member of a Jewish sect that out-wardly emphasized strict religious zeal and dedication and yet was also known for self-righteousness.

Perhaps Nicodemus came to Jesus by night because of the crowds that surrounded Jesus by day. Or perhaps Nicodemus wasn't quite ready to declare himself as "pro-Jesus." The two men probably spoke on the quiet rooftop of a private dwelling where evening breezes swept away the last heat of the day.

You'll need...

☐ blindfold

☐ Hula-Hoop

☐ adult actor to play Nicodemus

☐ copy of the "Nicodemus Script" (pp. 17-18)

☐ Bible-times costume, such as a robe and sandals, with a rich woven sash and head covering to denote the status of Nicodemus

☐ copies of the "John 3:16" handout (p. 21) on heavy paper

☐ craft knife

☐ markers

☐ 8-inch round blue balloons*

* Warning! Choking hazard—Children under 8 years of age can choke or suffocate on uninflated or broken balloons. Adult supervision required. Keep uninflated balloons from children. Discard broken balloons at once. Balloons may contain latex.

Nicodemus showed a favorable interest in Jesus, despite the fact that some of his compatriots wanted to kill Jesus. By seeking Jesus, Nicodemus stands out as a true God-seeker who would eventually associate himself with Jesus. Nicodemus appears only in John, here near the beginning and then toward the end (John 19:39), when he provides myrrh and aloes to prepare Jesus' body for an appropriate Jewish burial.

Theirs wasn't an easy first conversation. Jesus' initial statements went far beyond Nicodemus' ability to comprehend. Reading the passage and putting yourself in Nicodemus' shoes might be like sitting in an advanced math class where the teacher is talking, other heads are nodding, but you haven't the faintest idea of what's been said. Jesus often took this course in conversations, beginning with a statement that challenged what the listener could understand and then coming back with deep truths that reformed the listener's entire concept of the kingdom of God.

Such was the case with Nicodemus. Though Nicodemus was likely from an important aristocratic family, he came as the seeker and respectfully acknowledged Jesus as rabbi. Jesus didn't even wait for his guest to ask a question. He simply jumped into the incomprehensible statement that people needed to be "born again" to enter God's kingdom! However, Jesus also knew exactly what would spin the wheels of this learned man's mind. He knew the hunger of Nicodemus' heart and went straight to the answers this respected rabbi yearned for.

Jesus' words aren't always easy for us to comprehend, even after years of study. But he left them in his Word to speak to us in moments when we need them.

Come to the words of Jesus often. And, like Nicodemus, come hungry!

📖 Ezekiel 36:25-27

For Israelites who knew their Scripture—and Nicodemus did—Jesus' message of new life was not totally off the wall. Here in Ezekiel, the prophet mentions God giving a new spirit and new heart that's tender and responsive to those who are willing to be sprinkled with clean water.

This is the essence of redemption—to turn to God for new life. Jesus explained to Nicodemus this new way of living: that redemption would come through belief in Jesus, God's only Son. The writer of Hebrews would later describe it as "a new and life-giving way" (Hebrews 10:20) through belief in Jesus, the perfect Son and sacrifice.

All Together Now

While the *method* of salvation came as a complete surprise to the God-seeking Pharisee, the concept of salvation did not. What a humbling and utterly life-changing experience it must have been for the honorable Nicodemus to come face to face with the author of his salvation. For us, that long-anticipated privilege awaits us in heaven.

UNDERSTANDING YOUR KIDS

Eternal life? Christians are mocked by some in society for believing in something they say can't be scientifically proven. Your younger kids may soon encounter the pressure of being marked as "different" because they come from a Christian family that embraces the truth of God's Word.

Not only do we believe that Jesus was more than just another great prophet, we believe he was, and is, the Son of God, sent into the world so that those who believe in him will have eternal life. It's a joyous truth, not one to be uncomfortable with.

This lesson will help your kids accept the truth of John 3:16 in their lives—and find joy in sharing it with others.

ATTENTION GRABBER

Uggy-Buggy Tip Tag

Greet kids warmly. Early arrivers may help you inflate the blue balloons needed for the John 3:16 craft in Life Application. You'll need one balloon for each child plus extras in case of "poppers"!

Say: **You wouldn't mind turning into a bunch of little bugs, would you? You know, the little roly-poly kind? Here's how we'll do it: Squat down to your ankles. Now place your hands flat on the floor on either side of you to help you balance. In this position, walk like little roly-poly bugs. I'll call you Uggy-Buggies.**

Kids should be able to maneuver slowly.

One thing I've discovered is that Uggy-Buggies tip over kind of easily.

Gently tip over one of the Uggy-Buggies near you. Make sure the child has a soft landing.

Say: **Oops! Now this poor little Uggy-Buggy can't go anywhere. Bummer. But watch—I have just the thing to help.**

Encircle your fallen Uggy-Buggy with a Hula-Hoop and pull him or her upright. The fallen Uggy-Buggy will have to rock back and forth to help.

Ask:

• **Who wants to be the terrible enemy of the Uggy-Buggies?**

Choose a child volunteer.

Say: **You have a big advantage: You get to crawl. But you also have a big disadvantage: You can't see.**

Tie a blindfold around the volunteer.

Explain to kids how the game works. The blindfolded volunteer is the "Bumper." The Bumper remains with you while all the Uggy-Buggies scatter. When you let the Bumper go, the Bumper will slowly crawl around the room, listening and searching for an Uggy-Buggy. If the Bumper finds an Uggy-Buggy, the Bumper can bump the Uggy-Buggy off balance. Explain to kids that no big bashes are allowed—just gentle bumps.

If the Uggy-Buggy falls over, it plays "dead" until you come and bring it back to life with the Hula-Hoop. You'll slip the hoop around the fallen Uggy-Buggy and help the child up again. Then the Uggy-Buggy can take off and keep playing.

While the Bumper is searching, the Uggy-Buggies have to keep moving. The goal is to see how many Uggy-Buggies the Bumper can topple in two minutes. Say: **Are you ready? I'll blindfold the Bumper while you Uggy-Buggies scatter. Go!**

After two minutes, choose another Bumper and play again. This time, don't rescue any Uggy-Buggies with your hoop. Let play proceed until most of the Uggy-Buggies have been knocked over. Then call time and bring everyone together for discussion.

Ask:

• **Tell about which round of the game you liked best—and why.**

• **Describe how you felt when you thought you were going to get to play, but suddenly you were bumped out of the game.**

Say: **This is kind of like what happened to the people when Jesus explained who was going to get to go to heaven. People who were born as Jews** *thought* **they were going to heaven. But when Jesus came, he explained that things were different. A man named Nicodemus wanted to know how different—and what Jesus meant by the things he said. So one night he came to Jesus to find out. Let's find out who Nicodemus was, why he came to visit Jesus at night, and what he learned about having eternal life.**

BIBLE EXPLORATION

The Night Visitor (John 3:1-17)

Say: **Nicodemus likely came from a wealthy, aristocratic family that had been well-recognized in Jerusalem for several generations. And he served on the Sanhedrin—the Jewish ruling council.**

Surprisingly, Nicodemus was a Pharisee. Many Pharisees were bitter enemies of Jesus because they were jealous of his power and popularity. But Nicodemus was different. He didn't care so much about power and popularity. He just wanted to know God. His heart was hungry for knowledge of God. So, though he was a Pharisee, he recognized there was something quite special about Jesus. Unlike his Pharisee friends, Nicodemus wanted to know Jesus up close and personal. He wanted to ask Jesus questions that were burning in his heart.

Because Jesus was constantly surrounded by crowds of

Prep Box

Arrange for an older adult male volunteer to play the part of Nicodemus. Give him the "Nicodemus Script" (pp. 17-18) a week ahead of time to learn the script well. Have your volunteer waiting in the hallway for your cue to enter the room.

Teacher Tip

You may wish to create a nighttime scene in your room by dimming the lights, partially covering the windows and lighting safely placed jar candles or flicker lights.

people during the day, Nicodemus arranged to meet Jesus privately at night.

I don't want to give too much of what happened away. Let's see if we can catch Nicodemus as he returns from his late-night secret meeting with Jesus. Shh! I'll take a peek out the door.

Go to the door where your "Nicodemus" is waiting. As you begin to open the door, have the actor stride by your room.

All Together Now

Nicodemus Script

Nicodemus: Oh—you surprised me! Not many people are out in the streets at this time of night. Most houses are closed up tight.

Teacher: *(Speaking in hushed tones)* I'm sorry, sir. I didn't mean to frighten you. I have a group of kids here. They're followers of Jesus too. We'd love it if you'd come and tell us about your visit with Jesus.

Nicodemus: *(Looking around)* Is this a safe place?

Teacher: It is, sir.

Nicodemus: *(Relaxing)* Very well. I accept your invitation. *(To the kids)* Shalom, young disciples!

Teacher: Shalom, great teacher of Israel! It was so brave for you, a Pharisee, to visit Jesus. Don't most Pharisees consider Jesus their greatest enemy?

Nicodemus: Sadly, they do. I cannot judge them. I can only say that my heart has long burned with desire to speak to this young rabbi face to face. No one can do the things he does unless God is with him. Why, he may be mightier than Moses himself! God is in every word he speaks, in every miracle he performs. The spirit of God rests on him. He is...I believe he is the very Messiah we have waited for these hundreds of years! *(Pauses.)* I can hardly believe those words just came from my mouth!

Teacher: Your talk with Jesus must have been helpful!

Nicodemus: *(Hesitating)* Well, at first it I was completely confused. He spoke to me plainly enough, but his words made no sense at all.

Teacher: What do you mean?

Nicodemus: I hadn't even asked him a question yet, when Jesus declared, "No one can see God's kingdom without being born again." All I could think was, *I'm an old man! I can't go back inside my mother's belly and be born all over again!*

Teacher: Did Jesus explain what he meant?

Published in *All Together Now, Volume 3* by Group Publishing, Inc., 1515 Cascade Ave., Loveland, CO 80538.

17

Nicodemus: Yes. Eventually I understood. He said that we have to be born of water and of the Spirit. He was talking about a *heavenly* rebirth. Something only God can give us through the Spirit.

Teacher: I see. That makes sense.

Nicodemus: Yes! We don't know everything about the Spirit of God, but I understand that it works through Jesus. Look at how the Spirit of God is alive in everything he does! Jesus wants us to believe in him, because he comes from God the Father.

Teacher: So you believe that Jesus is God's Son?

Nicodemus: Yes, I do. Jesus told me so himself. God loved the world so much that he sent Jesus, his one and only Son to us. And ★ *everyone who believes in Jesus will have eternal life.* That means it's not enough to be born a Jew, which will be a big shock to my people, and many of them won't like it! We've always believed that we'd be included in heaven just because we're sons and daughters of Abraham. Now Jesus has made it plain that just being Jewish isn't enough. We must believe in God's Son, Jesus. That's what my Pharisee friends don't understand. They're so bound up in their own pride that they can't see that in Jesus, God's doing a whole new thing. Because of Jesus, the world will never be the same!

Teacher: Do you think you can persuade them to listen to Jesus like you did?

Nicodemus: *(Shaking his head)* I don't know. I just don't know. You see, we Pharisees think we have the answers about everything. None of us was expecting God to send the Messiah in this way. I hope I can get at least some of them to listen to me...to listen to Jesus. Now that I know this great truth, I want to share it with anyone who will listen. But faith only comes to those whose hearts are open.

Teacher: I see what you mean.

Nicodemus: The night grows later and later. I must return to my home. But it has been wonderful to meet you young disciples and tell you what I know of Jesus. Shalom, my young friends!

Teacher: Shalom, Nicodemus! Kids, say "shalom" to Nicodemus.

(Nicodemus exits.)

Ask:

• Why do you think Jesus' ideas were difficult for Nicodemus to understand at first?

• Tell about a time when you thought something was a fact, but it turned out not to be.

• What do you think it means to be reborn in Jesus?

Say: **The Jews spent hundreds of years thinking that they'd go to heaven simply because they were Jewish. Then Jesus came along and explained that going to heaven actually depended on being reborn through faith in him.**

In a way, the Jewish people were kind of like the Uggy-Buggies in the game we played earlier. The Jews thought that because of who they were, they'd be "in the game" when it came to heaven. But then they found out that it actually took faith in Jesus to give them eternal life with God. Without that faith in Jesus, they'd get bumped out of heaven. It was a lot for them to accept. But some people who saw Jesus do great miracles and listened to his teaching understood that ★ *everyone who believes in Jesus will have eternal life.*

LIFE APPLICATION

. . . .

John 3:16 to Go!

Say: **In speaking with Nicodemus, Jesus gave us one of the greatest and most-recognized verses in the Bible: John 3:16. Some call it "the gospel in a nutshell."**

We're not going to put this amazing verse in a nutshell; instead, we're going to make a super-fun way to share John 3:16 with others!

Distribute markers and copies of the "John 3:16" handout. Have your 8-inch blue balloons nearby.

Say: **Some people think John 3:16 is the most important verse in the whole Bible. While we read it aloud, please think about why some people think this.**

Ask a child volunteer to read John 3:16 aloud. Then have a second child volunteer read it aloud again.

Ask:

• What's the most important thing you hear in this verse?

Say: **Jesus didn't tell just anybody that he was God's only Son—he told Nicodemus, a man who belonged to a group of**

Prep Box

Cut the X's on the "John 3:16" handouts using a craft knife (you'll need one handout for each child). For extra durability, make copies on heavy paper. Inflate one blue 8-inch balloon per child, and have markers available.

Teacher Tip

Consider taping an extra blue balloon to the back of each handout in case the existing one meets with disaster before kids can share their handiwork.

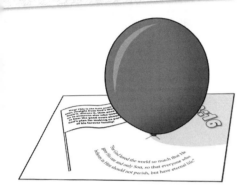

people who believed Jesus was their enemy. Jesus told this man that *anyone* who believed in him would have eternal life. Wow! This is news we don't want to keep to ourselves. That's why we're going to make this handout that you'll love sharing with your family and friends.

Have kids use markers to color the title, John 3:16, in colors of their choice. Then show them how to slip an inflated round blue balloon through the X to represent the world. Invite kids to sign their handouts if they wish.

COMMITMENT
Good News to Share

Say: **Now that we've made these cool John 3:16 handouts, the question is, how will we share them? If we put our heads together, I'll bet we can come up with all kinds of fun ways.**

Encourage kids to brainstorm creative ways they can share this good-news message with others.

CLOSING
Conversations With Jesus

Say: **We've learned a lot from the conversation Jesus had with Nicodemus. It would have been good to have been there that night, listening in as Jesus and Nicodemus talked. Imagine what it would've been like to sit on the rooftop of a Bible-times house, feeling the evening breeze stir across the sleeping city of Jerusalem, looking up at the stars and just *being* with Jesus and hearing his voice. Maybe we would even ask Jesus a question of our own!**

Before Jesus died and went to heaven, he told his disciples, "I will be with you always." Not in body, of course, but in spirit.

So this week or sometime when you're in a quiet place, I invite you to sit outside at night in a safe place with an adult—maybe on your porch or deck—and feel the evening breeze and look up at the same stars that shone down on Jesus and Nicodemus 2,000 years ago and quietly invite Jesus to speak to you. And then listen to that quiet voice of Jesus.

All Together Now

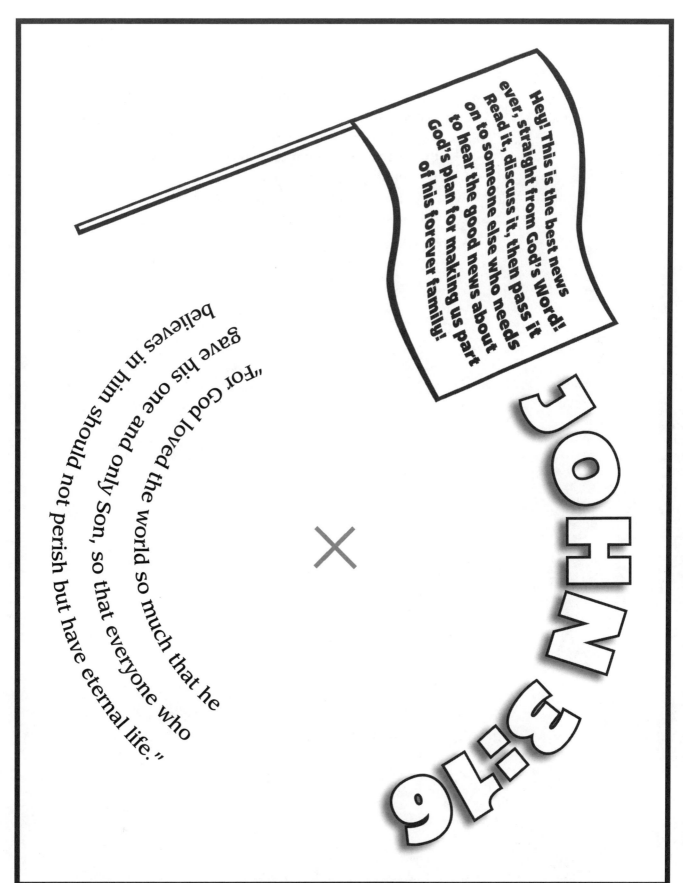

Hey! This is the best news ever, straight from God's Word! Read it, discuss it, then pass it on to someone else who needs to hear the good news about God's plan for making us part of his forever family!

JOHN 3:16

"For God loved the world so much that he gave his one and only Son, so that everyone who believes in him should not perish but have eternal life."

Ask:

• Where's a place you might do a quiet listening prayer in the evening?

Say: **Now let's close with an out-loud prayer of thanks for the things we learned in John 3:16. I'll start by praying, "Thank you, Jesus, that..." and someone can finish by praying something important you learned from John 3:16. Then I'll repeat my prompt and someone else can finish it.**

Thank you, Jesus, that...

Repeat as long as children add things they learned. Then close with your own expression of thanks.

My Father's House

You'll need...

- ☐ small bags of popcorn*
- ☐ tray
- ☐ 2 single-dollar bills
- ☐ 8 quarters
- ☐ clothesline or other soft rope, looped together
- ☐ copies of the "Windows on Worship" handout (p. 31)
- ☐ scissors
- ☐ pencils

* Always check for allergies before serving snacks.

LESSON AIM

To help kids realize that ★ *worship is a special time set apart to honor God.*

OBJECTIVES

Kids will

- ✓ role-play a worship service and experience a surprising interruption,
- ✓ participate in an interactive story about Jesus cleansing the Temple,
- ✓ create a unique folding envelope for recording responses to challenging questions about worship, and
- ✓ commit to and pray about approaching worship with good attitudes.

BIBLE BASIS

 John 2:13–22

"Gentle Jesus, meek and mild" does not make an appearance in this passage! In fact, the Jesus who presents himself here is so different from the Jesus we're used to, we almost need to take a step back, read the passage again, and ask: *What caused such a tremendous change in Jesus' demeanor?*

Without pretending to understand all of Jesus' motivations, we can see obvious forces at play here that would ignite Jesus' wrath.

Jesus cared much for the poor and little for religiosity. The keepers of the Temple cared much for show and little for the kingdom of God. This confrontation, though placed early in John's Gospel, had been brewing for some time. The keepers of Israel's holiest place had allowed God's house to become a well-oiled "den of thieves" (Luke 19:46). And Jesus, God's one and only Son, wasn't welcome on the premises.

Were you to walk through the Temple gate, you'd first encounter the court of the Gentiles where non-Jewish worshippers could approach the "mercy seat" from a respectful distance to offer prayers and worship to the one true God. The next place you would enter was the slightly higher court of the women, where Jewish women could worship and interact. Next was the court of the men, where only Jewish men were allowed. Finally, on the Temple grounds' highest plane was the court of the priests, where priests carried out sacrifices on Israel's behalf. Inside the court of the priests stood the Temple building. Its first room, the holy place, was several steps up from the court of the priests. Its inner room, the Most Holy Place, stood yet another several steps above that.

The most privileged in Israel's religious hierarchy could enter all the way in and all the way up to the Temple's Most Holy Place, which was considered to be the throne of God on earth. A priest entered this most holy place only once a year to present a sin offering on behalf of the nation.

The noise of money-changers and sellers of sacrificial animals that Jesus encountered was set up in the outermost court of the Temple—the court of the Gentiles. Yet it was God's purpose that the entire Temple Mount be holy—set apart—for worship. Business should've taken place outside the Temple. And it should've been carried out fairly.

Jesus, who had great compassion for the poor, saw his fellow Jews ripped off by vendors who plied their trade noisily within God's house. While an abundance of currencies were in use in Jerusalem, the Temple tax had to be paid in Temple currency, and the exchange rate was anything but fair to the people.

Other vendors sold animals appropriate for sacrifice at hugely inflated prices. Pilgrims coming to Jerusalem from outlying areas weren't able to bring their own "homegrown" animals. So the Temple vendors were more than happy to supply doves, sheep, and goats at far beyond fair market prices. This created a tremendous hardship for the poor but faithful Jews. It was, as we might put it today, a "racket." It's not hard to imagine Jesus' temper flaring when

All Together Now

he observed this kind of thing going on each time he entered his Father's house.

There's another, deeper issue that may well have been front and center in Jesus' mind. The Temple was his Father's house. Jesus' coming death and resurrection would soon do away with the need for Temple sacrifices altogether. But for now it stood in the hands of frauds and mercenaries. Wasn't it time for him to establish himself as the true heir and fulfillment of all God had promised? His actions left no doubt that he, Jesus of Nazareth, had authority to rule in his Father's house. His actions stated plainly: *Stand back! You who know nothing of my Father; see what he thinks of this! Give proper authority where it's due!*

📖 Isaiah 56:6-8

This beautiful passage tells of God's longing for the Temple to be a place of joy and a house of prayer for all nations. It evokes an image of God tenderly gathering in all the peoples of the world.

Rather than finding the Temple Mount a place of joy and a house of prayer for all nations, Jesus encountered the cacophony of greed. And the priests? They simply looked away. By overturning the money-changers' tables and running out the animals, Jesus demonstrated how woefully the guardians of Israel had failed to follow God's purpose. As God incarnate, Jesus dramatically cleansed the Temple of sinful practices and called to mind this Scripture, which laid out the Temple's original purpose.

UNDERSTANDING YOUR KIDS

Community worship involves a profound case of the wiggles for most kids—even when it's kids' worship designed specifically for them. There's gum to be chewed, secret jokes to be passed, giggle fits to be had, and chairs to be tipped so they nearly fall. Those leading take most of the responsibility for helping kids experience a "God moment."

This lesson dives into the ideas that we find great joy in God's presence and that we can each set our minds and hearts on seeking God and setting distractions aside as we approach God's house. Use this story of Jesus cleansing the Temple to encourage kids to approach worship with joy, with a purpose to set distractions aside and be gathered into the presence of God, who's more than ready to meet them.

THE LESSON »

ATTENTION GRABBER

Worship Interrupted

Greet kids warmly as they arrive.

Say: **To start off today we're going to set up something that looks like our worship service here at church. I'll need a couple of volunteers to lead songs together at our worship service.** Choose two or three child volunteers and send them off to decide which songs they'll lead.

Say: **The rest of us can sit like we would at our worship service.**

Sit in the back of the group so you can sneak away unnoticed. Support the kids leading the songs, but sometime into the second song, place your bags of popcorn on a tray, go to the back of the "worship area" and disrupt the singing by shouting: **Popcorn! Get your popcorn here! Fifty cents a bag. Tastiest popcorn in town. Step right up and get your popcorn! Don't wanna be without it! G-e-e-e-t your popcorn!**

When the children stop and look at you, ask: **What's wrong? Can't I sell a little popcorn if I want to? I mean, what's wrong with making a little money?**

Give kids a chance to respond to your interruption.

Pout a little for effect and say: **Hmm. Don't you think you're being a little hard on me? What's so bad about selling popcorn?**

Set the popcorn tray aside with assurances that you'll enjoy the popcorn later in class.

Say: **You might be surprised to know that Jesus encountered a situation something like this when he went to the Temple—like our church today—to worship. And he wasn't too happy about what he saw because ★ worship is a special time set apart to honor God. In today's passage, Jesus was just about as angry as we ever see him in the Bible! Let's go along with Jesus to find out why and what happened.**

BIBLE EXPLORATION

My Father's House (John 2:13-22)

Explain to kids that In Jesus' time the center of worship for all Jews was the Temple in Jerusalem. It held all the precious items from

---

Prep Box

Prepare a small bag of popcorn for each child. Hide the popcorn bags in a tote bag. Have a tray large enough to hold the bags of popcorn.

All Together Now

Jewish history long ago and was the most holy and sacred place imaginable.

The Temple was built on the highest spot in Jerusalem, called the Temple Mount. Not just anyone could visit all parts of the Temple. Tell kids you're going to take a "tour" to see what a visit to the Temple would be like.

Have kids help you drag a table against one wall of the room. Gather kids at the table and point to the top. As you give kids the "tour," gesture and encourage kids to use their imaginations.

Say: **This is the very highest part of the Temple Mount, inside the Temple building itself, behind a thick curtain. This was called the Most Holy Place and only the high priest went in here, and only once a year, to offer a sacrifice for the sins of the people.**

Now we step back and down several stairs to the first room of the Temple building. Lead kids in taking a few steps away from table. **Priests work here day and night to set out fresh bread offerings and to keep the lamps lit and the incense burning.**

Now we go backward out of the building and down more steps to the courtyard of the priests. Lead kids in taking another few steps away from the table. **Here the priests offered sacrifices to God.**

Another step backward finds us in the court of the men. Lead kids in taking one more step away from the table. **Regular Jewish men could come this far, but no farther.**

Now let's step backward, through a gate, and down just a bit. Lead kids in taking a few more steps away from the table. **This is the court of the women. Jewish women could come this far, but no farther. Treasuries and tall storerooms surround this large courtyard.**

Finally we're ready to back out through a low wall to the last and largest court: the court of the Gentiles. Lead kids in taking a few more steps away from the table. **People who were not Jewish but still believed in the one true God could come here to pray and worship. And *this* is where all the trouble started with Jesus.**

Invite the children to join you in a story circle.

Say: **In those days, people had to pay their Temple tax with special Temple coins. But the money-changers who sold the Temple coins cheated the people who came to worship. Let's see what that looks like.**

Give a one-dollar bill to two different children and prompt them to come to you and ask for Temple coins. Spread eight quarters out on your lap. When the first child comes and asks for Temple coins, give only two quarters in return for the dollar. Repeat with the second child. If they protest, wave them off to their seats.

Ask:

• **Describe what you saw that was wrong with how I exchanged the money.**

• **How do you feel about the way I did business?**

Say: **That's exactly how the money-changers in the Temple worked! They cheated people day after day. Right there in the court of the Gentiles that was meant for worshipping God.**

And then there were the animal vendors. You see, people who came from far away needed doves, lambs, and goats to offer as sacrifices. And each animal needed to be perfect. Back in the days of traveling by foot, people couldn't bring animals with them, so the travelers had to buy them in Jerusalem. But guess what? The animal vendors set up shop right there in the court of the Gentiles, a place that was meant for prayer and worship. Let's try to get an idea of the noises that would have been there.

Please coo like a bunch of doves. Let kids make dove sounds.

Now bleat like a bunch of goats. Let kids bleat like goats.

Now baa like a bunch of sheep. Let kids baa like sheep.

Now bicker like people arguing over prices. Let kids argue.

Gather kids' attention and say: **The Temple had been turned into a very noisy, stinky place.**

So this is what Jesus saw when he came into the Temple: tables of money-changers cheating people, cages full of noisy, smelly animals, and people arguing over their prices.

Jesus was *not* happy. In fact, he was downright *angry*! After all, the Temple was his Father's house, a place for worship and prayer. ★ *Worship is a special time set apart to honor God.*

Say: **Jesus drove the animals and their sellers right out of the Temple! People were amazed. They'd never seen Jesus act this way before.** Have kids stand up and decide whether they'll be a sheep, a goat, or a dove. Wave a looped clothesline around your head and begin driving the "animals" toward a corner of the room. Stop after a step or two and invite the kids to return to the story circle.

Then Jesus turned toward the money-changers. He scattered their money all over the floor.

Toss your money into the center of the circle and have kids with quarters do the same.

Say: **Then he turned over their tables and said, "My Father's house is a house of prayer, but you've made it a den of thieves!"**

People in the Temple could hardly believe their eyes—they'd never seen Jesus this angry. But they were glad, too. They knew about all the cheating that had been going on in God's Temple for years.

Ask:

• Why do you think what Jesus saw in the Temple made him so angry?

Say: **Jesus wanted everyone to know that ★ *worship is a special time set apart to honor God.* The Temple was to be a holy place, but the priests had allowed it to become a noisy marketplace where people who came to worship got cheated day after day.**

By his actions, Jesus was also teaching another important lesson: Because he was God's only Son, he had the right to say what should be going on in his Father's house.

LIFE APPLICATION
. . . .

Windows on Worship

Ask:

• What kinds of things do you think should be happening in a church, or God's house?

Say: **Jesus knew that it was God's plan to fill worshippers in the Temple with joy. We think about singing and praying and listening to God's Word, but we don't always think about joy. When we come into God's house to worship, we can expect God to be here with us. And there's joy in God's presence. Let's hear what the Bible has to say about that.**

Distribute the "Windows on Worship" handout. Ask a child volunteer to read aloud the passage from Isaiah.

Say: **Jesus quoted part of this passage when he cleared the Temple.**

Prep Box

Set out copies of the "Windows on Worship" handout, scissors, and pencils.

Ask:

• **Why do you think we experience joy when we worship God?**

Say: **Let's cut out and put together our Windows on Worship folders and then get together in groups to discover what else we've learned about worship today.**

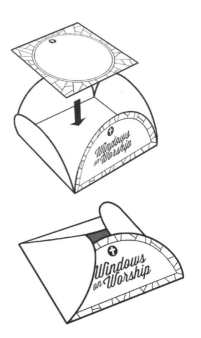

Have kids cut out the Scripture square and the folding envelope. Show kids how to lay the envelope blank side up and then fold in each of the half circles. When each half circle is tucked into the preceding half circle, the envelope will stay closed on its own. The Scripture square will tuck inside the envelope.

Have kids form groups of two or three. Say: **In your groups, take turns discussing each of the questions on your envelope flaps. Then write or draw what you've learned about worship from Jesus' actions and from the Scripture square on the blank part of your envelopes. Make sure everyone gets a turn to talk.**

After kids have had plenty of time to work and talk, ask a volunteer in each group to report their responses to the entire group.

COMMITMENT

One Thing to Do

Pass out the popcorn bags that you showed kids during the Attention Grabber.

Say: **Here's the popcorn I promised you! Help yourselves while we talk about one last thing.**

Think back to what kind of distraction this popcorn caused when we were having our mini-worship service earlier.

Ask:

• **How was my selling popcorn like or unlike what Jesus saw going on in the Temple?**

• **How might Jesus have reacted to what I was doing?**

• **Why did Jesus want to get rid of anything that took people's minds off God?**

• **Since we know that ★** *worship is a special time set apart to honor God,* **what can we do to turn away from distractions and draw close to God?**

Say: **Turn to a friend and tell one thing you'll do to focus on God the next time you're in worship.**

All Together Now

Windows on Worship

Jesus' surprising actions in the Temple caused quite an uproar! But what did you learn from what Jesus said and did that day?

Put the Windows on Worship mini-folder together with your teacher's help. Then get together in groups of two or three to discuss the questions. Write or draw your answers inside the folder and on the back of the Bible passage square.

Be prepared to be a new you in worship!

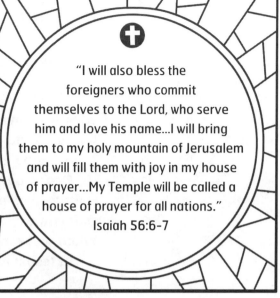

"I will also bless the foreigners who commit themselves to the Lord, who serve him and love his name...I will bring them to my holy mountain of Jerusalem and will fill them with joy in my house of prayer...My Temple will be called a house of prayer for all nations."
Isaiah 56:6-7

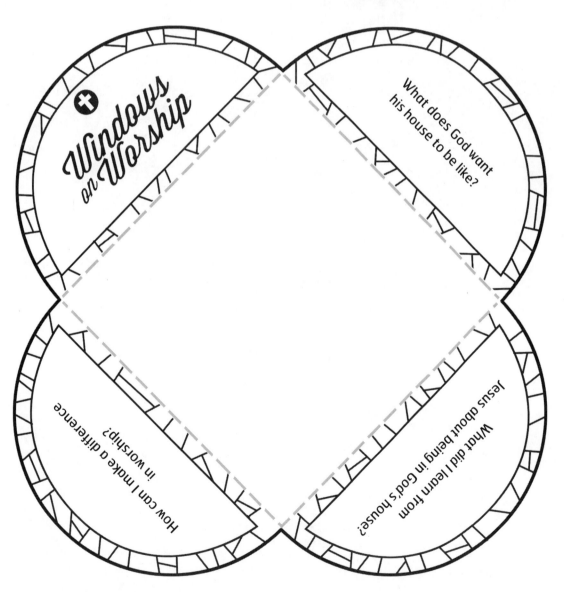

Windows on Worship

What does God want his house to be like?

How can I make a difference in worship?

What did I learn from Jesus about being in God's house?

Published in *All Together Now, Volume 3* by Group Publishing, Inc., 1515 Cascade Ave., Loveland, CO 80538.

CLOSING

· ·

Silent Response Prayer

Say: **Our closing prayer has a place for you to respond silently or in a whisper. When I pray, I'll leave a little time for you to do that. Then let's all finish together by praying,** *in Jesus' name, amen.*

Dear God, thank you for this Scripture that shows us that ★ *worship is a special time set apart to honor you* **and that you want to meet us there and fill us with your joy. When we worship you, help us focus on you by...**

In Jesus' name, amen.

All Together Now

Jesus Raises Lazarus From Death

LESSON AIM

To help kids realize that ★ *no matter what happens, God's timing is perfect.*

OBJECTIVES

Kids will

✓ do their best to prevent a "can-tastrophe,"

✓ work together on a circle-story presentation of Jesus raising Lazarus from the dead,

✓ create a paper craft featuring Psalm 30:5, and

✓ commit to trusting God's perfect timing even when things look like they're falling apart.

BIBLE BASIS

 **John 11:1-44**

What do you do when a good friend needs your help? Show up!

But in the case of Lazarus, Jesus chose not to. And his lack of attention to a dear family who had freely offered hospitality on many occasions was a mystery to many. Jesus lingered two days after receiving Mary and Martha's urgent message that Lazarus was seriously ill. In that interval, Lazarus died. How could Jesus be so uncaring of a family who cared so deeply for him? When Jesus finally arrived in Bethany, Martha said, "Lord, if only you had been here, my brother would not have died."

You'll need...

☐ 2 large boxes of rinsed and empty aluminum cans
☐ oscillating fan
☐ Hula-Hoop
☐ copies of the "Joy Stick" handout (p. 42)
☐ scissors
☐ glue sticks
☐ sturdy straws
☐ two 20-inch lengths of shiny curling ribbon per child

Our human desperation leaves us with tunnel vision. *Let the sick one live. Keep the bankruptcy from happening. Get us out of an unbearable situation. Bring a job—any job!* We can't fathom how a God who truly cares for us could ignore our pleas for help and mercy.

What we don't know, what we can't see or imagine, is the greater good God is working out by denying our immediate needs. What better thing will happen one, three, five, or ten years down the road?

Jesus had a clear picture of what was to come from his raising of Lazarus. It would be the last straw for the Jews opposing him in Jerusalem. They would realize that they could no longer have this young prophet on the loose doing astonishing miracles like this, drawing more and more followers to his side. In allowing Lazarus to die and raising him from the dead, Jesus knew that he was setting up his own imminent sacrificial death and resurrection. He was taking the long view—God's long view.

So even though Jesus' timing seemed awful, it was just right after all.

We who trust in God cling to this unshakeable hope: that what seems like disaster in the short term will prove to be one step in God's overarching plan in a future we can't yet fathom. God's timing is never off. God's care for us is never too late. Though we may feel crushed by the stress of life, if we keep clinging to our God, there's *always* joy in the morning.

Mary and Martha discovered this in the most dramatic and painful way. All of Jesus' followers would be plunged into this pattern during those two unthinkable days following his crucifixion. We will all encounter the challenge of looking for the larger mosaic of grace amidst the crushing pain of grief. For me, it's a rugged daily discipline to deal with the continual headaches and loss of competencies following my brain hemorrhage. It became a dreaded living reality for us as a couple when my husband reached the over-60, over-educated, and unemployable bracket.

Believe this, embrace it, never let it go: Joy comes in the morning. This is a promise from our unchanging God who cast the foundations of the universe.

📖 Psalm 30:5

How well do you know your God? How many times a week do you pray with all your heart and then listen to God with all your heart? It takes that kind of relationship to weather tragedy and

All Together Now

know from the depths of your being that joy will indeed come in the morning.

Jesus did not ignore Mary, Martha, and Lazarus; the sorrow and anger he felt upon meeting the two grieving sisters assures us of that. Jesus knew the front of the tapestry—God's greater plan— which would involve his own sacrifice and lead to the salvation of all people.

When you feel as deserted by God as Mary and Martha must have during those days when Jesus did not come, hang on to your God. Ask God to give you that inexplicable peace that comes because you know he's planned your days before the dawn of time. God delights over you, and loves you with an everlasting love.

God's timing is perfect, even when it seems everything is wrong.

UNDERSTANDING YOUR KIDS

Kids can readily get into the excitement of Jesus raising Lazarus from the dead. But denying the immediate, critical need in favor of something better further down the line? That's getting into foreign territory for all but your most spiritually sensitive kids.

And that's OK. Here you're laying the first stones of a deep spiritual foundation that other teachers, pastors, and life itself will build upon during the coming years. We start somewhere. The next time a child encounters this truth, it will lodge in a familiar niche because you have done the groundwork in establishing a neural network, a "hook" in the brain this concept can call home. More important, you're giving the Holy Spirit an opportunity to come alongside and illuminate God's own truth.

I've learned over the years not to fear laying out for children a truth that seems far beyond their reach. I can't count the number of times kids have surprised me by grasping far more than I expected, and by their comments, leading others along.

Use this lesson to assure kids that even when they feel that God has failed to show up to meet their needs, God's timing is always perfect.

THE LESSON »

ATTENTION GRABBER

Can-tastrophe

Give kids a warm welcome. Spread out your impressive collection of empty aluminum cans.

Say: **Look at all these cans. I'm wondering what kind of impressive tower you can build with them.**

Build your tower any way you like. Just let everyone contribute creative ideas and help in the building. I can't wait to see your creations!

Allow kids plenty of time for tower building. Offer encouraging comments as the work progresses. As you see the supply of cans dwindling, give a two-minute warning and then bring a halt to building when time is up.

Invite kids to show off the features of what they've built. Compliment kids' efforts.

Say: **Now I've got a bit of bad news for you. I'm sure you've all learned that life brings hard things—things we can't control. Here comes a hard thing.**

Set out an oscillating fan.

Say: **I'm about to turn this fan on your tower. Your job is to do everything you can to prevent a can-tastrophe. Will you be able to keep your lovely tower from falling down when the wind comes blowing in? If you work together, you might have a good chance. Let's see what happens!**

Begin with your fan on the lowest setting. Then turn it to medium, and eventually to high. Chances are kids will not be able to save their tower from the wind generated by the fan. You can control the fan's impact by moving it closer or setting it on a chair so the wind hits at a different angle. Keep working in this way until the cans fall down.

Say: **Oh, no! No matter how hard you tried, you couldn't prevent a can-tastrophe.**

Ask:

• **How did you feel when I changed the speed of the fan and moved it around?**

• **How is this experience like times when bad things happen in life, no matter how hard we try to keep them from happening?**

Say: **Sometimes we can't keep bad stuff from happening. When things fall apart, we might feel like God didn't show up or didn't care about us. But that's not true! Today we're**

Teacher Tip

If you have eight or more children in your class, you may wish to form two groups and have kids construct two towers. This isn't a competition! Encourage both groups to build their towers with cooperation and creativity.

All Together Now

going to learn that ★ *no matter what happens, God's timing is perfect.* Let's discover how that played out for friends of Jesus who lived in the small town of Bethany.

BIBLE EXPLORATION

Right on Time (John 11:1-44)

Say: **I need all of you to help me tell this story. It works like this.**

Have a classroom assistant stand facing you, holding a Hula-Hoop.

Explain that everyone will line up behind the Hula-Hoop. They'll help you tell the story in five parts, so you'll call a certain number of kids to step through the hoop for each part. Once kids step through the hoop, you'll tell what their roles are in the Bible story. Say that when you mention a person's name, you'll point to kids to play the role. Tell kids they won't speak, but will instead act out what you're telling. Remind kids that it doesn't matter if the role is of a girl or a boy—they just need to act out what you say.

Say: **When your part is finished, you can go to the end of the line and I'll call another group through the hoop. We'll keep going like that, with everyone taking turns acting out bits of the story. Just listen carefully for what you're supposed to do when it's your turn to act.**

Line up, and let's get going!

The words for kids to act out are printed in italic to help you emphasize them to kids. When a specific person is named, point to a child to act out that role.

Call three actors to be Mary, Martha, and Lazarus.

Say: **In the city of Bethany lived a small family of *three*— *two* sisters and *one* brother. They were a close family who *loved each other dearly*. And they loved Jesus, who'd often been their guest.**

One day Lazarus, the brother, *stayed in his bed on the floor*. He *shook and moaned and groaned*, too sick to get up. So the sisters, Mary and Martha, *sent word to Jesus*, thinking Jesus would come right away to heal their brother.

One day passed. Mary and Martha *looked for Jesus*. Lazarus still *moaned and groaned* on his bed.

Another day passed. Mary and Martha kept *looking for Jesus*. Lazarus kept *moaning and groaning*.

Finally Lazarus *stopped moaning and groaning*. He *became very still*. Mary and Martha *huddled together crying*, for they knew their dear brother had died. They wondered why Jesus hadn't come in time to heal him.

Thank the three actors and let them go to the end of the line. Call more actors to be Jesus, Martha, a Brave Disciple, and a few more to be Disciples.

Jesus was in a nearby city, *talking with some of his Disciples*. He said, *"Lazarus has fallen asleep. I'll go wake him now."*

The Disciples *looked confused*. They thought that if Lazarus had fallen asleep, it meant he was resting and getting better. So Jesus *explained*, "No, Lazarus has died. But I'm glad this has happened, for now you will really believe."

The Disciples *argued with Jesus* about going to Bethany. They knew Jesus had many enemies there and that it would be dangerous for him.

Then a Brave Disciple *spoke up* and said, "Let's all go with Jesus and die with him!"

Thank the actors and let them go to the end of the line. Call two actors to be Jesus and Martha.

Finally Jesus and Martha *met on the road* near Bethany. Jesus could see that Martha *was broken-hearted*. "Lord," she said, "if only you had been here, my brother would not have died."

Jesus *said*, "I am the resurrection and the life. Anyone who believes in me will live."

Martha *replied*, "I have always believed you are the Messiah, the Son of God."

All Together Now

Thank the two actors and let them go to the back of the line. Call two more actors to be Jesus and Mary.

Mary *came to meet Jesus* on the road. When she saw Jesus, she *fell at his feet and cried*.

When Jesus saw Mary and her friends crying, *he cried too*.

Mary *took Jesus to the grave* where they had buried Lazarus.

Call one child to be Lazarus. Have "Lazarus" lie under a table in the meeting area. Call the rest of the children through the hoop.

All of Mary and Martha's friends *joined Jesus* as he approached the grave of Lazarus. Then Jesus *called loudly*, "Lazarus, come out!"

Lazarus *came out of the tomb*, alive again. Everyone *rejoiced* that their friend was alive again! Many people *believed* in Jesus, for they knew that only the Son of God could perform such a miracle.

Lazarus *hugged Mary and Martha*. The sisters and brother *jumped for joy*.

Then Mary and Martha *talked*. They *realized* that Jesus hadn't come too late—he came just at the right time. ★*No matter what happens, God's timing is perfect*. Because such a crowd had seen Jesus raise Lazarus from the dead, even more people would believe in Jesus than ever before.

Have kids give themselves a big round of applause. Then invite them to join you in a discussion circle.

Say: **Let's think back to the beginning of class. Remember how hard you worked to keep your aluminum can towers standing when the fan began to blow?**

Ask:

• **How was that like the way Mary and Martha might have worked to take care of Lazarus, trying to help him get well?**

• **How do you feel about Jesus not coming right away when his friends needed him?**

• Put yourselves in the place of Mary, Martha and sick Lazarus. How might you feel when day after day passed without Jesus showing up?

Say: **Mary, Martha, and Lazarus were really counting on their good friend Jesus to come help them at an important time. What they didn't know was that Jesus had something even better in mind. They still had to learn that ★** *no matter what happens, God's timing is perfect.*

Ask:

• What good things happened because Jesus waited to come to Bethany?

Say: **Mary, Martha, and Lazarus believed in Jesus as the Savior of the world. But they hadn't seen him do anything as amazing as raise someone from the dead. They also hadn't seen how very much Jesus really loved them and cared about their feelings.**

When Lazarus came out of the grave at Jesus' command, a whole crowd of people saw Jesus' love and power and work and believed in him for the first time. Then those people told others, so the good news about Jesus spread far and wide.

LIFE APPLICATION
. . . .
God's Good Timing

Say: **What we're talking about today isn't the easiest lesson to learn—even for adults. Mary and Martha felt terrible when their brother died. Lots of times in life terrible things happen even when we do our best to prevent them.**

Place the Hula-Hoop around yourself.

Say: **I invite you to think of something that may seem like a bad thing, but might actually be part of God's more important—and better—plan. For example, one thing that might make people feel terrible is if they don't get a job they really need. But God's timing might be to give them a much better job a little later.**

Ask:

• **Tell about a time you wanted something to happen, but it didn't.**

• **Describe how the situation made you feel.**

Place the Hula-Hoop around a child volunteer who wants to

All Together Now

share. Have other volunteer kids join the first child in the hoop until everyone who wants to share has been able to. If the Hula-Hoop gets too crowded, let other kids just share where they are.

Say: **It helps to know that lots of us have felt that way. But here's something we can all remember: God works in his own time. He knows the bigger picture of what's best for us. So we may not understand why something doesn't happen when we think it should, but God knows and he works things out for us in the end.**

COMMITMENT
. . . .
Joy Stick

Say: **It was a hard time for Mary and Martha when Lazarus died. They probably weren't thinking,** *This is hard, but God will make something great come out of it in the end.* **One way we trust God is by remembering the promises he gives us in the Bible. I have a great promise from God for you today that will remind you that ★** *no matter what happens, God's timing is perfect.*

Lead kids to your craft area where you've set out copies of the "Joy Stick" handout, scissors, glue sticks, sturdy straws, and two 20-inch lengths of shiny curling ribbon per child. To create the Joy Sticks, lead kids through the steps listed on the handout.

Invite kids to tell where they will keep their Joy Sticks at home.

CLOSING
. . . .
Keep Believing

Have kids each take an aluminum can from the ones used in the Attention Grabber and place the straw of their Joy Stick in the can.

Say: **The aluminum can represents the hard things that come in life. No matter how hard you tried, you couldn't prevent a can-tastrophe. The Joy Stick reminds us to keep trusting God's promises, because ★** *no matter what happens, God's timing is perfect.*

Put God's promise over your heart, cross your hands over it, bow your head and silently pray, "God, I trust you."

Pause a few moments, then close with, ***in Jesus' name, amen.***

Prep Box

Before class, make a sample Joy Stick for kids to see.

Teacher Tip

You may want to have kids create two Joy Sticks—one to keep and one to give away to someone who needs encouragement. Invite kids to brainstorm who might benefit from receiving a reminder of this great promise from God.

Joy Stick

When difficult things happen, use this promise from God as a reminder that God will bring better things in the future.

1. Fold stars together where the two points meet and cut them out at the same time.

2. Rub a glue stick around the edges of the back of one of the stars. Do not rub glue along the bottom of the star.

3. Glue the two stars together so the print sides are showing on front and back.

4. Rub a glue stick thoroughly around the top 1/2 to 3/4 inch of a study straw.

5. Insert the glued part of the straw into the center of the bottom opening between the two stars. Hold the straw in place until the glue dries.

6. Finish by folding two 20-inch lengths of shiny curly ribbon in half. Rub a glue stick on the folds. Insert the folded ribbons on each side of the straw. Hold them in place until the glue dries.

JOY
COMES WITH THE MORNING
Psalm 30:5

THIS IS GOD'S PROMISE TO YOU!

Published in *All Together Now, Volume 3* by Group Publishing, Inc., 1515 Cascade Ave., Loveland, CO 80538.

The Most Important Things

LESSON AIM

To help kids realize that ★ *as Jesus prepares a place for us in heaven, he wants us to remain in his love.*

OBJECTIVES

Kids will

✓ do their best to solve tricky brainteasers,

✓ enjoy a meal similar to one Jesus shared with his disciples,

✓ make a souvenir booklet in response to Jesus' teaching, and

✓ share their booklets with friends.

BIBLE BASIS

 **John 14–16**

At the Last Supper, Jesus filled his disciples with reassurance and guidance for the grueling days that were to follow. Unfortunately, these beautiful pastoral passages of Jesus are often skipped in children's ministry resources because it seems that there's not enough time to cover all the impactful events between Palm Sunday and Easter.

Now's a great time to give kids a peek at the intimate things Jesus shared with his closest followers just before his arrest. Knowing that he had just a short time with his disciples, Jesus capped his nearly three years of shared life with them

You'll need...

☐ plastic tablecloth

☐ breadmaker with a just-finished loaf of bread (if you don't own a breadmaker, ask a friend to do this for you). If you can't use a breadmaker, use a fresh loaf of unsliced bread*

☐ knife

☐ plate of grapes cut into small bunches*

☐ plate of strawberries cut in half*

☐ jar candles

☐ lighter

☐ napkins

☐ wet wipes

☐ copy of the "Verse Strips" handout (p. 49)

☐ scissors

☐ copies of the "Supper With Jesus Souvenir Booklet" (p. 51)

☐ pencils

* Always check for allergies before serving snacks.

by packing John 14 through 17 with culminating truth, warnings, encouragement, and prayer. Things that before Jesus had spoken of metaphorically, he now spoke of plainly, so when the disciples' world fell apart on Friday afternoon they would have his final words and prayer for them as a touchstone of hope until the glory of Easter morning.

Though Jesus had told his disciples time and again that he was going to his death, he told them once more that he was going away. This time he assured them that his going away would not be permanent; in fact, he was going to prepare a place for them—a place in his Father's house! And when it was time, he would come back for them and they would always be together.

It was the custom of many a Hebrew young man who was taking a bride to build a room or series of rooms that attached to the courtyard of his father's house. In this way the family home grew to a sprawling structure with plenty of room for everyone. This might have been the image Jesus was planting in his disciples' minds—we don't know for sure.

Jesus' important, unspoken message? *I'm not deserting you. I'll never desert you. Though I may leave for a little while, I'm getting things ready for you and then I'll come back and take you to be with me always. Until then, remain in my love.*

Jesus explained that there was no greater love than to lay down one's life for one's friends. The disciples were about to witness this greatest act of love. Jesus wanted them to see it as just that—an act of great love, not a defeat—and then to honor their friendship with him by loving each other.

📖 Psalm 27:13

Through the historic narratives of their people, the disciples knew what it was to have their hopes hang on the outcome of a battle, the whim of an emperor, or an interceding miracle of God.

Jesus' farewell address would call to mind great psalms of faith such as this one that little Jewish boys would have put to memory in their synagogue studies before the age of 12. Jesus' address pressed them to call on these memories as they faced the great tests the next few days would bring.

UNDERSTANDING YOUR KIDS

Abandonment is high on kids' list of fears. They can easily identify with these segments of Scripture pulled from the longer context of John 14–17. They'll love knowing that Jesus is preparing a place for them, too, and until then, here are their instructions: Love each other.

As Jesus tenderly cared for his disciples, he tenderly cares for all of us—especially the young among us. *You'll never be abandoned or forgotten; I'm coming back for you.* Good words for us, and our kids, to carry with us every day of our lives.

THE LESSON »

ATTENTION GRABBER

Too Hard to Figure?

Greet kids warmly as they join you. Invite kids to do a few warm-up exercises because they're going to need all their brain-power to do the activity. Have kids do 15 jumping jacks, run in place for one minute, stretch their fingers high in the air, and then stretch all the way down to their toes. Have them follow these exercises by a few deep breaths.

Rub your hands together and say: **Now you're ready to take on any challenge I can throw at you! I've got some tough brainteasers here. You're welcome to huddle and work on the answers together. Let's see how many of my brain-teasers you can figure out together. Are you ready?**

Ask these questions aloud one by one, giving the kids plenty of time to consult with each other.

✓ **There's a skateboard trick that's not possible to do. What is it called?**
   Impossible.

✓ **What's as light as a feather, but even the strongest man cannot hold it for more than a few seconds?**
   His breath.

✓ **Can you name three days in a row without naming Sunday, Monday, Tuesday, Wednesday, Thursday, Friday, or Saturday?**
   Yesterday, today, tomorrow.

✓ **What's full of holes, but still holds water?**
   A sponge.

✓ **How far can you walk into the woods?**
   Halfway. After that you're walking out.

If kids are able to come up with any of the answers, congratulate them.

Say: **Know what? These brainteasers were just about too hard to figure out on your own. We needed the guidance of someone wiser to solve them.**

As we get ready for today's Bible exploration, you'll see that the disciples were about to find themselves in need of lots of wise guidance from Jesus. They were soon to face a

All Together Now

situation that was too hard for them to figure out on their own. So Jesus sat down with them at a meal and explained some very important things. Let's get ready to join them!

BIBLE EXPLORATION

. . . .

Supper With Jesus (John 14:1-3; 15:9-14, 17)

Say: **I'd like to invite you to a special meal today. It was the last meal Jesus shared with his disciples before he was arrested. Jesus had a long talk with his disciples at this meal, because he knew he would die soon. He was about to leave his friends, and he knew they wouldn't be able to figure out all the scary things that would happen in the next few days. Jesus wanted to give them all the help he could.**

In Jesus' time, people ate at low tables and sat on pillows on the floor. Let's set up our meal on the floor like a picnic.

Invite kids to help you spread out a plastic tablecloth, and set out napkins, the fresh bread, a plate of grapes cut into small bunches, and a plate of strawberries cut in half. Dim the room and light your picnic area with jar candles. Have kids clean their hands with wet wipes.

Say: **Jesus blessed bread and wine and shared it with his friends. This bread smells good! Now we can share it, just as Jesus and his disciples did.**

Pass the fresh bread around your group, encouraging each child to tear off a piece. Pass grapes the other way. Remind kids to enjoy the juiciness of the grapes. If kids ask, explain that you're saving the strawberries for a little bit later.

Say: **This meal was part of the Passover feast. Jesus and his disciples were in Jerusalem to celebrate the feast together. Jesus knew that within a few hours he would be arrested. Let's listen in on what he told them.**

Distribute Verse Strips 1 through 3 to child volunteer readers. After the first reading, ask the volunteers to read their verses again. The verses are all reprinted here for you to reference.

> *Don't let your hearts be troubled. Trust in God, and trust also in me. There is more than enough room in my Father's home. If this were not so, would I have told you that I am going to prepare a place for you? When everything is ready, I will come and get you, so that you will always be with me where I am.—John 14:1-3*

> ## Prep Box
> Bake, or have a friend bake for you, a loaf of bread in a bread machine so it's done as your lesson begins and its fragrance fills your meeting area. To prepare for the Bible Exploration, remove the bread from the pan and cut it in a few large slices. Kids will each tear a piece of bread for themselves. Also cut apart the strips of the "Verse Strips" handout to be distributed during the story.

Ask:

• **What good news do you hear in these verses?**

• **What do you think it will be like when Jesus welcomes us to heaven?**

• **Describe how you feel knowing that Jesus is preparing a special place for *you* in heaven.**

Say: **Let's hear more of what Jesus had to say.**

Distribute Verse Strips 4, 5, and 6 to child volunteer readers. Again have kids read through the sequences of verses twice. The verses are reprinted here for your convenience.

I have loved you even as the Father has loved me. Remain in my love. When you obey my commandments, you remain in my love, just as I obey my Father's commandments and remain in his love. I have told you these things so that you will be filled with my joy. Yes, your joy will overflow!—John 15:9-11

Say: **Jesus said that he remained in his Father's love by obeying his Father's commandments—in other words, doing what his Father told him to do.** ★*As Jesus prepares a place for us in heaven, he wants us to remain in his love.*

Ask:

• **Does that work the same with our parents here? How do we "remain in their love by obeying them"? Explain.**

• **How would obeying Jesus fill our lives with joy?**

Distribute Verse Strips 7 through 10 to child volunteer readers and repeat the double-reading sequence. The verses are reprinted here for your convenience.

This is my commandment: Love each other in the same way I have loved you. There is no greater love than to lay down one's life for one's friends. You are my friends if you do what I command. This is my command: Love each other.—John 15:12-14, 17

Ask:

• **In what ways had Jesus shown his love for his disciples?**

• **In simple terms, what do you think Jesus is saying in this passage?**

Say: **Jesus often emphasized the importance of loving each other. That's why I've saved strawberries for our last treat.**

Pass the plate of strawberries and ask:

• **When you look at a strawberry half, what does it remind you of?**

Verse Strips

1 Don't let your hearts be troubled. Trust in God, and trust also in me.
John 14:1

2 There is more than enough room in my Father's home. If this were not so, would I have told you that I am going to prepare a place for you?
John 14:2

3 When everything is ready, I will come and get you, so that you will always be with me where I am.
John 14:3

4 I have loved you even as the Father has loved me. Remain in my love.
John 15:9

5 When you obey my commandments, you remain in my love, just as I obey my Father's commandments and remain in his love.
John 15:10

6 I have told you these things so that you will be filled with my joy. Yes, your joy will overflow!
John 15:11

7 This is my commandment: Love each other in the same way I have loved you.
John 15:12

8 There is no greater love than to lay down one's life for one's friends.
John 15:13

9 You are my friends if you do what I command.
John 15:14

10 This is my command: Love each other.
John 15:17

Published in *All Together Now, Volume 3* by Group Publishing, Inc., 1515 Cascade Ave., Loveland, CO 80538.

Say: **Strawberry halves look a lot like hearts. As we enjoy our strawberries, let's remember the last verse we heard: Love each other!**

Have kids help you clear the food; then wipe and fold the tablecloth.

LIFE APPLICATION
. . . .

Supper With Jesus Souvenir Booklet

Say: **When we go someplace special, we often like to bring back a souvenir. Because the Bible records Jesus' words so carefully, we were just able to share a meal that was a lot like the final supper Jesus shared with his disciples. That's something you can always remember.**

Show kids the sample booklet you made before class and explain that it's a lot easier to write or draw in the souvenir booklets before folding them, so they'll do that part first. Tell kids they'll work in pairs to read and discuss the verses and questions on each page.

Once kids have drawn or written their responses, lead them through the cutting and folding instructions printed on the handout. They'll be delighted to see their flat sheets of paper become diamond souvenir books.

Demonstrate how to turn a front *and* a back page in the diamond souvenir books at the same time in order to progress through the pages of the books.

Have kids help clean up the craft area and then bring their souvenir books and join you in a circle on the floor.

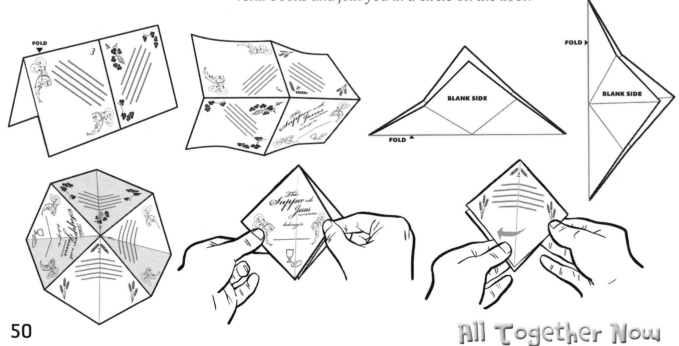

All Together Now

Supper With Jesus Souvenir Booklet

What important memories did you make during your supper with Jesus? Record them by drawing or writing in this cool souvenir booklet.

Once you've filled out the booklet, form it into a diamond by cutting out the big square and folding it carefully on the center lines.

Open it, and fold it in half diagonally. Open it again, and fold it in half diagonally the other way.

Open it again. Using your thumbs and forefingers, grab one of the centerline folds about halfway down each side of the fold. Push down and in gently until the center of the booklet pops up.

Brainstorm three different ways you could "love each other" this week.

Love each other.
John 15:17

This is my command:

What does it look like to remain in Jesus' love?

I have loved you
even as the Father has
loved me. Remain in my love.
John 15:9

3

2

There is more
than enough room in my
Father's home. If this were not so,
would I have told you that I am going to
prepare a place for you?
John 14:2

What kind of place do you think Jesus is
preparing for you in heaven?

This
Supper with
Jesus

SOUVENIR
BOOKLET

belongs to

Published in *All Together Now, Volume 3* by Group Publishing, Inc., 1515 Cascade Ave., Loveland, CO 80538.

51

COMMITMENT

Tell a Partner

Say: **Find a friend you have *not* talked to about your souvenir booklet. Please get together with that person right now.**

First, take turns sharing what you wrote or drew in your booklets. Then tell each other one way you'll remain in Jesus' love this week.

CLOSING

Huddle Prayer

Ask kids to get in a tight huddle.

Say: **Let's close our time together in prayer. Dear Jesus, thank you that we can remain in your love, not only when we're in a tight huddle of Christian friends, but throughout the week. In your name, amen.**

All Together Now

In the Garden

LESSON AIM

To help kids realize that ★ *praying can help us stand strong.*

OBJECTIVES

Kids will

✓ try to meet the challenge of not bending,

✓ play the role of sleepy disciples as Jesus prays,

✓ make a paper Prayer Garden with Psalm 105:4 and prayer prompts, and

✓ use the Prayer Garden for the closing prayer.

BIBLE BASIS

📖 **Matthew 26:36–46**

In this lesson we tackle one of the most poignant stories of the New Testament. We witness Jesus, who was both fully God and fully human, struggle with the awful night and day that lay ahead of him.

Jesus knew the humiliation and torturous death that would happen so quickly after his arrest. He also knew he easily could call legions of angels to his rescue. He knew the everlasting implications of his sacrifice, and yet the *fully human* part of him struggled.

The New Testament doesn't give us the full picture of the brutality of Roman rule. That's not what the writers set out to do. It's likely that Jesus had witnessed many instances of

You'll need...

☐ artificial plants (perhaps borrowed from other areas of the church) to create a garden setting

☐ glue sticks

☐ scissors

☐ copies of the "Prayer Garden" handout (p. 60)

☐ craft knife

☐ half-sheets of construction paper in assorted colors

☐ markers

Roman brutality, often carried out summarily by the roadside. Yet brutality was the opposite of who Jesus was.

Jesus knew that the Sanhedrin—the purported guardians of Israel—would break their own rules and meet at night to trump up charges that would somehow qualify him for the death penalty of the Romans. That on the next day at 3 o'clock when the *shofar* sent its wild call from the tower of the Temple through the streets of Jerusalem to announce the hour of sacrifice, he would have become the sin of the world, abandoned by his heavenly Father.

In this Scripture we see the fully human side of Jesus struggling with this last act of obedience. He would stand alone before Caiaphas and his false witnesses whose stories were so poorly patched together that no two matched. Jesus would be whipped, mocked, beaten, and spat upon. Alone he would stand before Pilate, alone he would carry the cross on wounded shoulders and stumble through streets below his Father's house. He alone would bear the wounds of the crucifixion, slowly suffocate, and die.

Being raised on or having grown accustomed to this story has a way of numbing us to its dreadful reality. I can remember my brother singing the lovely anthem "I Walked Today Where Jesus Walked." That music would transport me and make me long to have been there *for* Jesus, *with* Jesus, *in the garden*. And that's where I'd love for you to find yourself before you teach this lesson.

You see, I can't just sit down and write a lesson for kids about Jesus in the Garden of Gethsemane without first being with him there myself—through hours of meditation on this Scripture, grappling with my own Gethsemanes, researching piles of books and dozens of pictures of the Kidron Valley, possible sites of the garden, images of ancient olive trees, and yes, listening to several versions of "I Walked Today Where Jesus Walked" on YouTube.

We modern thinkers love to obtain knowledge, put it under a microscope and observe it, rub our chins and say, "hmm," and then congratulate ourselves on putting more stuff into our vaults of expertise. As the English writer G.K. Chesterton humorously put it, "The poet only asks to get his head into the heavens. It is the logician who seeks to get the heavens into his head. And it is his head that splits."

But Jesus came from the ancient world. He taught profound truths in simple picture phrases. As God he was *Rock, Fortress, Deliverer, Healer, Provider, Alpha and Omega, I AM.* As human he was breakable flesh facing down the final hours until he would become the sacrificial lamb. Alone. Afraid. Pleading his Father for a way out. Three times asked, three times denied, finding his best friends asleep. Yet somehow in that crushing green grief of the garden, Jesus found strength in those prayers to do what he was born to do.

📖 **Psalm 105:4**

So many times Scripture urges us to look to God and to seek God's face. In this verse from Psalms, we're asked to continually search for God. Those who seek him will surely find him and receive strength to stand strong in the stresses of life. Jesus took these appeals to heart throughout his ministry, often going off to be alone with God in prayer.

Jesus needed these times of spiritual encouragement. So do we. But I find myself too often thinking of prayer as an obligation, whereas really it's a time of refreshment when God readjusts my perspective, reminds me of his priorities, and gives me the strength to stand strong. Prayer is as necessary to our souls as water is to our bodies. Enjoy lots of it this week!

UNDERSTANDING YOUR KIDS

Can you remember as a child biting off a big task, being full of enthusiasm at the beginning of it, but then crumpling before you were halfway through? That's so typical of kids—starting out with every good intention, and then throwing their hands up in discouragement long before the finish line.

This week's Scripture lets kids see that even Jesus was susceptible to despair when his life was on the line, and that his lifeline became his prayer relationship with his Father. They'll learn that ★ *praying can help us stand strong.*

Developing a solid prayer relationship is a lifelong pursuit. Many adults don't even fully get it. Use this lesson to encourage your kids to use prayer as their lifeline to God, to help them stand strong in God's will through everyday circumstances as well as life's traumas.

THE LESSON »

ATTENTION GRABBER

No Bending Allowed

Greet kids warmly as they arrive and say: **I need a volunteer for a difficult challenge.**

Choose a lightweight, younger child volunteer. Have your child volunteer stand stiff and straight with elbows bent at the sides of the body.

Say: **Now, no matter what I do, stay stiff and straight. No bending allowed.**

You or another adult can pick up the child by the elbows, carry him or her across the room, and set the child down. Ask kids to judge whether your volunteer stayed perfectly stiff.

Say: **Okay, let's have another volunteer.**

This time choose a medium-sized child. Instruct this child to stand with feet slightly spread apart and elbows bent. Stand close to one side of the volunteer. Assign two of your strongest kids to stand equally close to the other side.

Say: **We're going to rock you gently from side to side. You may not bend or give in any way. Stand completely stiff.**

Begin by tipping the volunteer just a bit, and then both you and the other "tippers" will gradually step farther apart. After a few rocking motions, give this volunteer a round of applause.

Ask for a third child volunteer. Choose a confident child of medium size.

Say to the volunteer: **You'll stand stiff and straight with your arms down at your sides.**

Instruct the rest of the kids to form a shoulders-touching circle around the volunteer. Ensure you have stronger kids and adult volunteers all around the circle.

Say: **When I give the signal, we'll start passing you around the circle. Just rock back on your heels and let us pass you around. If you stay perfectly stiff, it'll be easy!**

Once the child is stiff, gently pull him or her back toward you and then begin "passing" the child.

Say: **Well executed, everyone! You've really shown what a strong bunch of kids you are!**

Invite everyone to join you in a circle on the floor.

Ask:

• **Describe how easy or difficult it was to stay strong in this experience.**

Teacher Tip

When rocking your volunteer, have the rest of the kids stand in front of and behind the volunteer as spotters.

Teacher Tip

Once one child has been passed around the circle, others will want to try it. You'll need to decide whether you have enough adults or older children to make this happen safely. If you do, by all means, let everyone try!

All Together Now

• How was this like or unlike standing strong against problems in life?

Say: **If you make a plan, such as finishing your homework before you play with friends, take a stand and be firm about following through on that plan. Or if you make a promise to your parents, stand firm and follow through.**

Sometimes, though, something that seemed a good idea at first can become overwhelming. For instance, what if you discover your homework is going to take twice as long as you thought? Or the promise you made to your parents is too difficult for you to do alone? We all get tired and start to crumple a bit. If we don't have the strength to carry on, we feel like giving up.

Ask:

• **When have you ever felt like giving up on something?**

Be ready to share your own experience when you needed extra strength from God to carry on.

Say: **The Bible tells us about how this happened to another person. We're also going to learn that ★ *praying can help us stand strong*. You're going to help me tell the Bible passage for today—and we'll find out what happened.**

BIBLE EXPLORATION
· ·

Sleepy Disciples (Matthew 26:36-46)

Say: **After a special supper with his disciples, Jesus led them outside the house where they were staying in Jerusalem, through a city gate, and down into a cool valley. Night had fallen and the disciples were tired, but they knew Jesus was leading them to a quiet garden across the valley on the lower slopes of the Mount of Olives. It was a favorite place of Jesus, outside the busy city, and he and the disciples had been there often. A few stars sprinkled the sky as they began to climb out of the steep valley and up the Mount of Olives.**

Jesus was strangely quiet. It was his way to teach as they walked together, but this night everything felt a bit different. Jesus had been different at supper, too. The disciples were curious, to be sure, but in the end being tired won out over being curious.

Now I'll pause our lesson because we need a garden.

Prep Box

Place several large artificial plants to stage an area of the room as the Garden of Gethsemane.

Let kids work together to arrange their garden in any way they like. Guide them to one end of the garden and say: **The disciples were glad when Jesus told most of them to sit down as soon as they arrived at the garden. But he asked his three closest friends, Peter, James, and John, to come a little farther into the garden with him. He asked these three friends to stay awake and keep watch with him, for he was filled with sadness. Then Jesus went off a bit farther by himself to pray. Jesus knew that ★** *praying can help us stand strong.*

Unfortunately, Peter, James, and John were just as tired as everyone else. Within moments, all the disciples were sound asleep.

From now on, you're the sleepy disciples.
Ask:

• Where will you sleep in our lovely garden?
Allow kids to arrange themselves in sleeping postures.

Say: **I'm sorry to tell you that what happened next is incredibly sad.**

Walk among kids' sleeping forms as you say: **Jesus knew that his enemies were almost ready to arrest him. He knew that before the next day was over, he would die on the cross. He prayed and prayed to God that he wouldn't have to suffer the awful things that were about to happen. Each time when he came back to see whether his friends were keeping watch with him, he found them asleep. Each time he prayed to his Father in heaven for a way out, he came away knowing that he must do his Father's will and die on the cross to make a way for everyone to know God.**

Shh, now, sleepy disciples. Don't say a word, but sit up and join me here in the center of the garden. Hear how the account of Jesus ends.

When the kids join you, read in a hushed voice:

Slee-py disciples,
Your Savior needs a friend,
Jesus in the garden now,
Knows his life must end.

Slee-py disciples,
Why so heavy-eyed?
Jesus in the garden now
Needs you by his side.

All Together Now

Slee-py disciples
Don't you have a care?
Jesus in the garden now
Cries to God in prayer.

Slee-py disciples,
Hear your Savior groan?
Jesus in the garden now
Trembles all alone.

Slee-py disciples,
Won't you stay awake?
Jesus in the garden now
See his shoulders shake?

Slee-py disciples
You who've been so still,
Jesus in the garden now
Ready for God's will.

Fold your hands and bow your head for a few seconds. Then say: **And now you know what happened with Jesus in the garden of Gethsemane.**

Ask:

• **Describe how you felt when you listened to this account of Jesus praying in the garden.**

• **Why do you think Jesus wanted his friends close to him that night?**

Say: **Jesus was God's only Son, but he was also born of a woman—Mary. Because he was both God and human, Jesus understands us completely.**

Ask:

• **Why do you think it was hard for the human side of Jesus to stand up to what was about to happen to him?**

• **How did spending time talking to God help Jesus?**

Say: **Jesus knew that even in the scariest situations,** ★ *praying can help us stand strong.* **Taking time to be with God puts a new perspective on things. It helps to remember that God loves us more than we can imagine, that God's in control, and that his power is greater than anything in this world. And knowing that changes everything!**

Prayer Garden

Make your own garden of prayer you can visit any time!

1. Cut out the garden base below.
2. Cut the three trees apart. Fold each one in half at the top and cut out both halves at the same time.
3. Slip the bottom tabs of a tree through a slit in the base. It doesn't matter which tree goes in which slit.
4. Fold the tabs toward the base. Put glue on the tabs, and stick them to the back of the base.
5. Glue the base to a half-sheet of construction paper. You can fold the construction paper and garden in half for safe carrying.

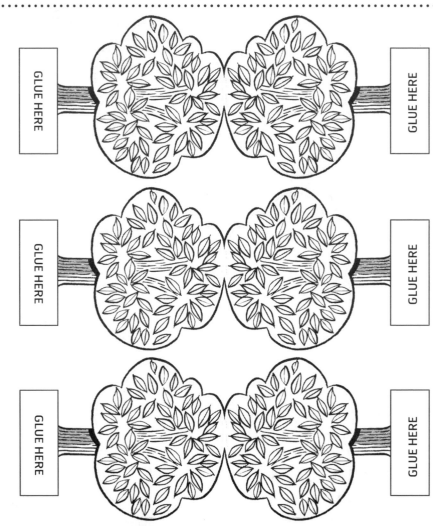

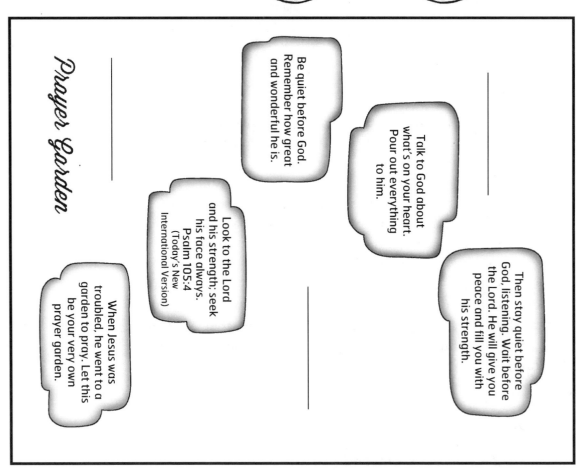

Prayer Garden

Be quiet before God. Remember how great and wonderful he is.

Talk to God about what's on your heart. Pour out everything to him.

Look to the Lord and his strength; seek his face always. Psalm 105:4 (Today's New International Version)

Then stay quiet before God, listening. Wait before the Lord. He will give you peace and fill you with his strength.

When Jesus was troubled, he went to a garden to pray. Let this be your very own prayer garden.

LIFE APPLICATION

Prayer Garden

Say: **Knowing that** ★ *praying can help us stand strong* **even in the hardest of times, I'd like each of you to have your own Prayer Garden. This one will just be made of paper, but you can keep it with you and "walk" through it whenever you need to. Let's get started.**

Lead kids to your craft area, and guide them through the instructions on the handout to complete their Prayer Gardens. Have kids each write their name on their completed project. Demonstrate how to fold the Prayer Gardens in half on the slit line for the middle tree for safe carrying.

Invite kids to help you clean up the craft area as they finish.

COMMITMENT

A Walk in the Garden

Say: **Let's take a walk through our Prayer Gardens together.**

Invite child volunteers to take turns reading what's printed on the stepping stones.

Ask:

• **After reading through this, what ideas do you have about how** ★ *praying can help us stand strong*?

Say: **Turn to a partner and talk about when you might use your Prayer Garden at home.**

CLOSING

Prayer on the Stepping Stones

Say: **Let's use the stepping stones in our Prayer Gardens for our closing prayer. Please form a circle. We recognize this time and place as our own Prayer Garden.**

Lead everyone in a step to the left and say: **God, we look to you for our strength. We're seeking your face.** Pause.

Prep Box

Use a craft knife to open the slit lines for the trees on each handout. Make a "Prayer Garden" to show to the kids. Set out scissors, glue sticks, half-sheets of assorted construction paper, and copies of the "Prayer Garden" handout (p. 60).

Teacher Tip

Let kids use markers or other materials at hand to color their Prayer Gardens.

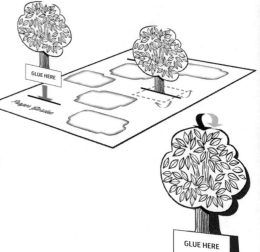

Lead everyone in another step to the left and say: **God, we'll pause here for a moment to remember how wonderful you are.** Pause.

Next, lead everyone in a step to the right. Say: **Now we'll pause quietly, God, so each of us can tell you something that's on our heart.** Pause.

Next, lead everyone in another step to the right. Say: **Thank you for listening to us and filling us with your peace. We believe that because you listen to us and help us,** ★ *praying can help us stand strong.* **In Jesus' name, amen.**

A King for a Day

LESSON AIM

To help kids realize that ★ *Jesus came to be king of our hearts.*

OBJECTIVES

Kids will

✓ make newsprint costumes for a game of Who Do You Think I Am?,

✓ find hidden palm branches to reenact the story of Palm Sunday,

✓ create a digital viewer of their Palm Sunday experiences, and

✓ participate in a Hosanna! prayer.

BIBLE BASIS

 **John 12:12-19**

The feast of Passover filled Jerusalem to many times its usual population. It was one of three feasts that male Jews within a certain number of miles were required to attend, but in reality, Jews from everywhere strove to attend. Various scholars have estimated that this geographically tiny city bulged to hold anywhere from 250,000 to 1,000,000 people! And they attended in a religious frenzy, ever aware of the heavy hand of Rome even as they celebrated God's deliverance from the heavy hand of Pharaoh.

The Romans sent extra soldiers for this event from as far

You'll need...

☐ newsprint

☐ several colors of construction paper

☐ chenille wire

☐ glue sticks

☐ scissors

☐ masking tape

☐ staplers

☐ flashlight

☐ 4 copies of the "Palm Branch" handout (p. 68) on green paper

☐ marker

☐ olive oil

☐ cotton balls

☐ blanket

☐ CD of Palm Sunday praise songs

☐ CD player

☐ copies of the "Phone Flash" handout (p. 72)

away as Caesarea to keep the crowds under strict control. It was the way of the Romans to parade their intimidating forces through the streets, the golden eagle at the head of the vanguard of mounted soldiers, followed by well-armed, well-disciplined foot soldiers marching shoulder to shoulder in strict time.

Under Roman occupation, the Jews found themselves in constant stress. Their religion demanded total obedience to God. The Roman emperors demanded the same. Both Jews and Romans were very proud of their different traditions and histories. Some Jewish leaders tried to live with Roman rule as best they could and asked the people to be patient, knowing that all empires ultimately collapse. Other Jewish leaders rallied the people to take up the fight, and to take up the fight *now*. Thus, conflict was inevitable, and various Jewish groups and coalitions intermittently revolted against Roman rule. The last revolt happened about 40 years after Jesus' crucifixion, when the Romans ruthlessly crushed the rebellion and destroyed the Temple.

Rome's hand, therefore, was a heavy one. Its taxes kept the people poor. Governors remained in Jerusalem only as long as they kept the people quiet. The feuding Herods had been discarded and replaced by the likes of Pontius Pilate. As Prelate of Judea, Pilate also lived in Caesarea, but was expected to come with his troops to oversee this troublesome Jewish holiday and keep the peace.

So if you've always thought of Palm Sunday as an easy breezy, bright sunshiny day filled with butterflies and flowers, step back and take a fresh look. Jesus was about to enter a smoldering situation, and by the manner of his entrance, he ignited a firestorm of conflict.

By entering the city on a donkey, Jesus fulfilled Old Testament prophecies regarding the coming king, particularly Zechariah 9:9. The donkey was an animal of peace in contrast to the Romans' war horses, and in Eastern eyes the donkey is not looked down on or laughed at. King Solomon rode David's donkey into Jerusalem for his coronation (1 Kings 1:33). To the Jewish leaders who opposed Jesus, this entrance was an in-your-face statement by Jesus that he was the Messiah and they would have to deal with him as no less. Jesus had raised Lazarus from death; made his royal entrance to the city; and gone to the Temple and knocked over the money-changers' tables, drove out the animals for sacrifice, and accused the priests in charge of allowing his Father's house to become a den of thieves.

Further, the waving of palm branches and laying of coats in the road was a welcome reserved for kings as we see in 2 Kings 9:13 and also when Simon Maccabaeus entered Jerusalem after a great victory. Palm branches were also a key part of the feast of the Tabernacles and are mentioned in Psalms. Since the time of the Maccabees, palm branches had indeed become a nationalistic symbol of Judaism. As recently as 2011, with Middle East tensions simmering, Egypt refused to export the branches of date palms to Israel to celebrate their feasts.

While leaders in Jerusalem looked with dread at a rival to political power, Jesus himself looked forward to a week of suffering, sacrifice, betrayal, and the ultimate triumph. That ultimate triumph continues today as he became, and is, King of all hearts for all time.

📖 Zechariah 9:9

In his triumphal entry into Jerusalem, Jesus fulfilled this prophecy. The Jews knew this Scripture and knew exactly what Jesus was doing. That's why they cried, "Hosanna!" which means, "Save us!" They looked to this astonishingly gifted teacher and healer to save them from Roman rule. Little did they understand that before the week was out, he would become the Lamb of God and make the ultimate sacrifice to become King of their hearts.

UNDERSTANDING YOUR KIDS

Our Bible point, ★ *Jesus came to be king of our hearts,* begs the question of what rules kids' hearts before Jesus enters the picture. Think about the chatter you hear from kids before and after your time together for the lesson. Do you know how your kids spend their spare time?

There's no substitute for getting to know the kids you teach. That knowledge allows you to take the material presented here and tweak it to the level of their walk with Jesus. Sometimes I've been known to feel inwardly cranky when kids show up early or don't get picked up until well after others are gone (oh no!), but that precious individual time can be key in understanding what's going on in a child's life.

Use this lesson to help kids understand that Jesus could have taken the easy road and become the popular earthly king the crowds wanted him to be. Instead, he took the hard road, and he did it for us.

THE LESSON »

Who Do You Think I Am?

Greet kids warmly and help them form groups of two to four. Make sure each group has an older and a younger child.

Say: **Your job is to use the items on the table to make a costume that'll transform someone in your group into a famous character. It can be someone from history or a cartoon character—any famous character you'd like. You'll have just a few minutes to make a convincing costume, but keep your plans a secret! We'll see whether other kids can guess who your famous character is.**

Circulate among groups to help them settle on ideas and get started. Encourage kids to be modest in their costume planning. Explain that they're not looking for perfection, just recognition. Be available with staplers and steadying hands to help complete the costumes.

Give a two-minute warning so kids can bring their costume designing to completion, and then call time.

Say: **It's time to put your costumed characters on display and play, Who Do You Think I Am?** Ask for a volunteer character to step into the spotlight.

As each costumed character comes forward, shine a flashlight on him or her (but not in the eyes, of course). Then have the character ask: *Who do you think I am?*

Allow kids several guesses before you begin supplying clues. Applaud each character before calling the next one forward.

After each of the characters has been identified, have pairs or trios help their characters remove their costumes. Have everyone join you in a circle, and ask:

• **What's the best costume you've ever worn—and what made it so good?**

• **Tell what you think is fun about wearing costumes.**

• **How is wearing a costume different from what we wear in everyday life?**

Say: **When we wear costumes we get to pretend for a little while that we're somebody we're not—maybe somebody big and scary or beautiful or with superpowers. But when we take off the costumes, we're back to being our real selves.**

When Jesus entered Jerusalem on Palm Sunday, a lot of people assumed he was somebody he wasn't. They thought

Prep Box

Prepare a table with the following materials: newsprint, several colors of construction paper, chenille wire, glue sticks, scissors, and rolls of masking tape. Also have staplers and a flashlight on hand.

All Together Now

he'd come to be the new king of Jerusalem and king of Israel. That's what it *looked like* to them. But that was sort of like seeing Jesus in the wrong costume. Soon they would come to understand that ★*Jesus came to be king of our hearts.*

BIBLE EXPLORATION

. . . .

Find the Palms! (John 12:1-19)

Say: **Uh-oh! I don't have what I need to begin our story! Oh—I remember. I hid it somewhere in the room before you got here. You're going to need to find it for me. Here's a clue for you: It has something to do with today being Palm Sunday.**

Turn the kids loose to search for Palm Branch 1. When a child finds it, have everyone gather in a circle on the floor. Have the finder read or get help reading the message on the palm branch out loud: "Just a dab."

Say: **Just a dab? Let's see what that means.**

Explain that before Jesus entered Jerusalem, he stayed with his good friends Mary, Martha, and Lazarus in the little town of Bethany. Bethany was just about two miles from Jerusalem. After dinner Mary took a bottle of expensive perfume and poured it on Jesus' feet and then wiped his feet with her long hair. The perfume filled the entire room with its beautiful fragrance.

Say: **In Bible times, pouring expensive oil on someone was a way of honoring or anointing that person. Jesus took Mary's offering of perfume as a beautiful gift. I'd like to anoint each of you with a bit of olive oil on one of your hands to show that you're a precious child of God.**

Pour olive oil on a cotton ball and dab some on each child's hand. As you do so, look each child in the eye and say: **You are a precious child of God.**

Ask the children to hold that thought in their minds, bow their heads, and keep their eyes tightly closed as you hide Palm Branch 2 (you may want to use tape for this). When you return to the circle, release the kids to find it. Ask the finder to read or get help reading the message: "Where's the donkey?"

Say: **Something tells me we'll see a donkey before too long...we'll just have to wait and see!**

On Palm Sunday morning, just a few days before the

Prep Box

Cut out each of the palm branches from the copies of the handout. On the fronts, number them one through four. Write on the back of the branches as follows:
1. Just a dab.
2. Where's the donkey?
3. Branch out!
4. Got praise?
Hide Palm Branch 1 in an obscure place in your meeting area. Keep the rest of the Palm Branches with you to hide as the story proceeds.

Teacher Tip

Be aware that some children may feel uncomfortable being anointed. If a child doesn't want to be anointed, move on to the next child without comment.

Palm Branch

Passover feast, the city of Jerusalem was brimming with people who'd come from far and wide to the feast.

Ask:

• **When have you been in a crowd so big that you had to push your way through, or where you thought you might lose your mom or dad?**

Say: **That's exactly what it was like in Jerusalem. The population swelled to several times its normal size for the Passover feast. And not just with Jews. The Romans sent extra soldiers to ensure the crowds stayed under control. The Roman soldiers paraded through the streets making sure everyone could see their leaders mounted on war horses and their famous marching legions stomping in time. The Romans were determined to keep the Jews under control by showing their strength.**

Everyone show me the big muscles in your arms and say *GRRR!* **That's right. Now stand up and do it again.** *GRRR!* **Now face somebody and do it even louder.** *GRRR!*

Yeah! That's what the Romans were like!

But while the Romans were parading their might through the streets, a very different kind of parade was beginning in the little town of Bethany. Jesus sent his disciples to find a donkey that had never before been ridden tied up next to a house. When someone asked why they were taking it, the disciples answered, "The Lord needs it."

They took the donkey to Jesus and threw their robes over it so it would be comfortable for Jesus to sit on.

Now **we need a donkey.** Choose an older, sturdy child to play the part.

Have that child get down on all fours, and throw a blanket over his or her back.

Say: **Next we need someone to represent Jesus!**

Choose a small child volunteer. Place that child on the "donkey's" back.

Say: **And so, Jesus started out for Jerusalem. Now, he wasn't on a war horse, but he was fulfilling a great prophecy that the Jews knew about. Listen carefully to this Scripture. It's Zechariah 9:9:**

Rejoice, O people of Zion! Shout in triumph, O people of Jerusalem! Look, your king is coming to you. He is righteous and victorious, yet he is humble, riding on a donkey—riding on a donkey's colt.

Say: **When all the crowds in Jerusalem saw Jesus coming, riding on a colt, they thought he was their king. They thought he was coming to throw out the Romans and free Israel. So they started shouting, "Hosanna! Blessed is he who comes in the name of the Lord!"** Have kids shout with you. **They cut palm branches from trees and took off their cloaks and laid them in the streets. Everyone cheered as Jesus rode into Jerusalem.**

Thank your donkey and Jesus actors. Then have kids cover their eyes as you take your tape and hide Palm Branch 3 quickly. Have the child who finds it read or get help reading the clue on the back: "Branch out!"

Say: **I know what that means! We're supposed to find branches to wave, just like the people in Jerusalem did.** Take kids on a quick excursion outside. Tell them the rule that no one runs ahead of you. When you find a tree or a bush, have all kids *gently* grab a limb without pulling it off and shout, "Hosanna!"

When you return to your room, have kids stand in a tight huddle with their eyes closed while you hide Palm Branch 4. Have the finder read or get help reading the clue on the back: "Got praise?"

Say: **Let's sing our praise to ★*Jesus, who came to be king of our hearts.***

Lead kids in your favorite Palm Sunday praise songs, such as "Hosanna," "King of Kings and Lord of Lords," "Blessed Is He Who Comes in the Name of the Lord," "All Hail King Jesus" or another favorite. Then gather everyone in a circle.

Say: **The people who greeted Jesus didn't have things quite right. They thought Jesus would be a king on earth who'd throw out the Romans and rule in Jerusalem and make their lives a lot easier. But that isn't what God had in mind. This great parade happened on Sunday, but Jesus knew that by the next Friday the crowds would turn against him and he would die. Then he would rise again and conquer death because ★*Jesus came to be king of our hearts.* He came to make a way for us to be part of God's forever family. And that is good news!**

LIFE APPLICATION

Phone Flash

Say: **Jesus' story is pretty incredible. And it's good to tell your friends and families all about it. Let's make it easy for you by putting pictures right on your phones!**

Lead kids to your craft area where you've set out scissors, glue sticks, and copies of the "Phone Flash" handout (p. 72).

Have kids follow these easy steps to complete their phones.

✓ Cut out the slides and tabs as one solid piece.

✓ Cut out the front and back of the "phones" separately.

✓ Carefully punch scissors through the window in the front of the phone, and then trim the rest of the window.

✓ Rub a glue stick below the dotted lines on the back of the phone. Stick that side to the unprinted side of the front.

✓ Slide the slides through the open sides of the phone. Use the tabs to pull them back and forth.

Say: **How do you like having your own "smart" phone? You've just made a great device for telling lots of people that ★** *Jesus came to be king of our hearts.*

> ## Prep Box
> Make a sample phone from the "Phone Flash" handout (p. 72) so kids have an idea of what they're making.

COMMITMENT

Phone Share

Ask kids to find friends and practice using their newly created "phones" to tell each other about Palm Sunday.

Encourage kids to explain to each other that Jesus didn't come to be king of Israel, but instead ★ *he came to be king of our hearts.*

Ask:

• **What are creative ways you can use your phones to tell your families and friends about Palm Sunday?**

Phone Flash

Share the exciting events of Palm Sunday with your family and friends on your very own "phone!"

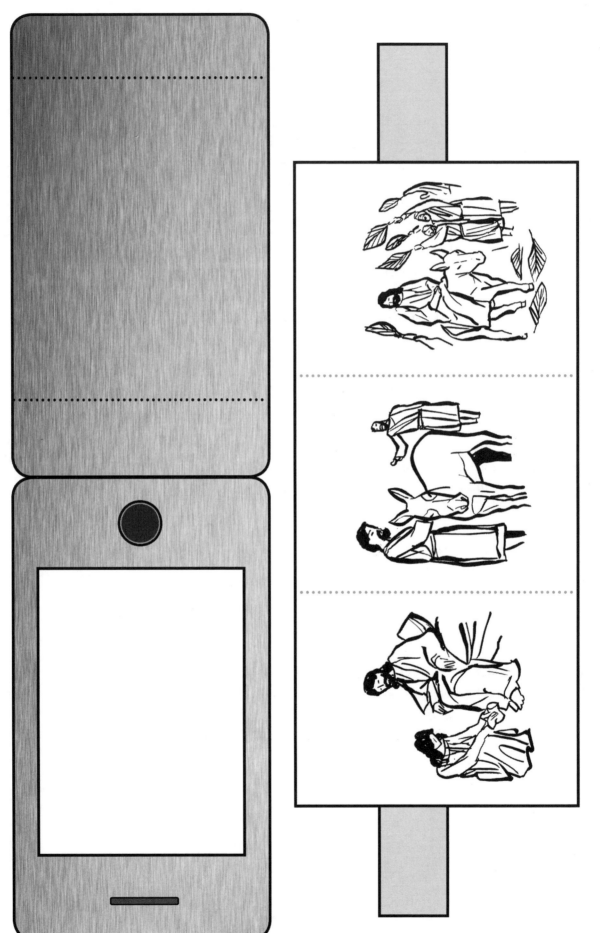

CLOSING

....

Hosanna Prayer

Say: **Let's make our closing prayer by remembering what Jesus did for us on Palm Sunday. Your part of the prayer is to say, "Hosanna!" which means, "Save us!" after I've said something in prayer. So whatever I say, you follow with "Hosanna!" Let's pray.**

Jesus, by your word the heavens and the earth were formed.

Hosanna!

Jesus, you came to earth to show us what God is like.

Hosanna!

Jesus, you died for us and then rose again.

Hosanna!

Jesus, now ★ *you are king of our hearts.*

Hosanna!

Hosanna in the highest!

Hosanna!

In Jesus' name, amen!

Breaking News: Jesus Has Risen!

You'll need...

- ☐ Hula-Hoop
- ☐ copies of the four "News Team Assignments" (pp. 80-81)
- ☐ large newsprint tablet
- ☐ markers
- ☐ microphone or paper towel tube
- ☐ copies of the "Jesus Is Alive Lily" handout (p. 83)
- ☐ scissors
- ☐ glue sticks
- ☐ three cotton swabs per child
- ☐ green and yellow markers
- ☐ pencils
- ☐ CD of Easter praise songs
- ☐ CD player
- ☐ optional: video recording cell phone with attachment to laptop

LESSON AIM

To help kids believe that ★ *Jesus is alive!*

OBJECTIVES

Kids will:

- ✓ create pretend headlines that are too good to be true,
- ✓ present a simulated live news broadcast about Jesus' resurrection,
- ✓ make "Jesus Is Alive!" lily paper sculptures, and
- ✓ sing Easter praise songs.

BIBLE BASIS

 Matthew 28:1-10; John 20:3-9, 19-20, 24-28

We're the people of God because we share a story and a vision.

The story is this: God created the universe, the world, and the people in it for fellowship with their Creator. Sin entered the picture and we spoiled the fellowship. God made a special people through a covenant with Abraham, and gave them laws to keep them safe and holy. The people failed God, and the separation between God and people grew as wide as before. Finally, in great compassion, God sent Jesus to earth. Both fully God and fully human, Jesus walked and taught among us, to give us a picture of God's true love. At the height of his popularity, Jesus chose to go the way of the Cross, giving his own life as a permanent sacrifice for sin. On the third day he rose from the dead, conquering death and opening the way to God for all who would believe in him.

Alleluia! ★ *Jesus is alive!* The old covenant of law and death is broken; a new covenant of love and life now stands in its place. And if that doesn't shake your soul to its very core, there's something wrong with your shaker!

Our vision? To share the good news of Jesus' victory over death until he comes again, sweeps the earth clean, and establishes a new heaven and new earth where he reigns forever at the right hand of God. In the meantime, God sent us the Comforter, Counselor, the one who walks beside and advises us, the very Holy Spirit of God, to lead us into all truth, to encourage and guide us along our path as we walk as followers of Jesus.

Sweeping, isn't it?

Sit back, take a deep breath, and ask the Holy Spirit to help you take in our story and our vision. The Easter story isn't just another Bible story. It's the central point in history—the fulfillment of all that came before, and the hope of all that comes after.

 **Isaiah 53:1–11**

In this Scripture, you'll find a stunning, blow-by-blow foreshadowing of Jesus' sacrificial death and the fruit of his resurrection. In Psalms, you'll find many other direct prophecies to the manner of Jesus' death, particularly in Psalm 22. Also note Psalm 16:10, Psalm 34:20, Psalm 35:11, Psalm 41:9, Psalm 68:18, several verses in Psalm 69, Psalm 118:22-23 and 26.

As Jesus himself said, "Anyone with ears to hear should listen and understand" (Matthew 13:43).

UNDERSTANDING YOUR KIDS

Believing the Resurrection is the big jumping-off point of faith for Christians of all ages.

If kids attend public school, they're probably being taught about the scientific method. But Jesus' resurrection isn't something that can be repeated or tested in a blind study. It's one of those "by faith" references in Hebrews 11.

Young hearts open sweetly to the faith stories of the Bible. They readily embrace the fact that "God loves us so much that…" In my years of teaching I've had only one fifth-grader pop up and say,

All Together Now

"That's just a myth." It was heartwarming to see his fourth- and fifth-grade choir mates gently explain that just because the stories of the Bible can't be explained by modern reason doesn't make them untrue!

I've always been taken aback by people who have the arrogance to make themselves and their knowledge the standard by which to measure all things. But as any astronomer, microbiologist, geneticist, or physicist will tell you, the more they learn, the more they acknowledge how little they know.

Use this lesson to help kids joyfully acknowledge *by faith* that ★ *Jesus is alive!*

THE LESSON »

ATTENTION GRABBER

Too Good to Be True!

Welcome kids warmly and wish them a happy Easter.

Say: **To start off today, we're going to take turns making up news that's too good to be true. I'll start.**

Lay a Hula-Hoop in the middle of the meeting room and say: **My too-good-to-be-true news is that there'll be no school for the rest of the year!**

Lead kids in cheering. Say: **Form groups of two or three and help each other dream up more news that's too good to be true. I'll give you a couple of minutes. When I call you back, you'll get a turn to stand in the middle of the Hula-Hoop and announce your too-good-to-be-true news.**

Have kids take turns standing in the Hula-Hoop and announcing their news. Have the group applaud after each announcement.

After all groups have announced their too-good-to-be-true news, ask:

• **Which too-good-to-be-true news was most difficult to believe? easiest to believe?**

• **When have you heard too-good-to-be-true news in your life?**

Say: **Our Bible passage today is about news that was too good to be true. But in this case, God was involved, and with God anything is possible, so the news was absolutely true! The news is that ★ *Jesus is alive!* At first the news sounded too good to be true, even to Jesus' own disciples. But soon more and more people saw for themselves that it was true. Let's find out what happened.**

BIBLE EXPLORATION

Breaking News: Jesus Has Risen!

(Matthew 28:1-10; John 20:3-9, 19-20, 24-28)

Say: **I'm sure you can remember a time when some important, life-changing event happened.**

Ask:

• **Describe what happens on TV when important news breaks.**

All Together Now

Say: **Lots of times news stations switch from one reporter to another. One reporter will tell one part of the story, another reporter might interview a person involved in the story, and another reporter might show close-up pictures of what happened.**

Well, when Jesus rose from the dead it was *huge* **news! And there were lots of different people involved. So I've taken important Scriptures about Jesus rising from the dead and made them into assignments for four different news teams. When you're assigned to a news team, study your Scripture together and then decide how you'll present it on our live newscast here in our room. For instance, you may plan to interview one or two of the people in the story. Or you may choose one person in your group to report while the rest of you act it out in the background. You may want to do a visual report by drawing "live pictures" on newsprint.**

However you decide to tell your part of the story, make sure you capture the excitement of that first Easter as more and more people discover that Jesus really is alive.

Help kids form four news teams. If four teams are too many for your group, leave out the fourth report about Thomas and simply make three news teams. Make sure you a have a mix of children of all abilities in each news team. Hand out the "News Team Assignments" (pp. 80-81). Circulate among the groups as they prepare their assignments, offering encouragement and ideas as necessary.

Check to make sure each group is nearly ready to present before you call out a two-minute warning. Then call time and have the news teams present their reports in order. They can use the microphone or paper towel tube to imitate newscasters if they wish.

After each news team presentation, encourage kids to ask questions of that news team about their report.

Say: **Normally I have several questions for you throughout our Bible stories. Today, however, I'd like you to go back into your news teams and come up with interview questions about today's story. Your interview questions have to be** *thinking* **questions to get people talking. OK reporters, back to your teams!**

Give news teams two to three minutes to develop one or two questions. Have someone who didn't have a speaking part in their news presentations ask the entire group questions. Encourage kids to give each question thoughtful discussion.

Teacher Tip

Option: If you have a phone with video or access to a video recorder, record each news team's presentation. After all the presentations, allow kids to watch them together on your phone or laptop.

EXTRA! EXTRA!
READ ALL ABOUT IT!
BREAKING NEWS!

News Team 1
THOSE INVOLVED: Two Marys, Angel, Jesus
SCRIPTURE: Matthew 28:1-10

28:1 Early on Sunday morning, as the new day was dawning, Mary Magdalene and the other Mary went out to visit the tomb.

2 Suddenly there was a great earthquake! For an angel of the Lord came down from heaven, rolled aside the stone, and sat on it.

3 His face shone like lightning, and his clothing was as white as snow.

4 The guards shook with fear when they saw him, and they fell into a dead faint.

5 Then the angel spoke to the women. "Don't be afraid!" he said. "I know you are looking for Jesus, who was crucified.

6 He isn't here! He is risen from the dead, just as he said would happen. Come, see where his body was lying.

7 And now, go quickly and tell his disciples that he has risen from the dead, and he is going ahead of you to Galilee. You will see him there. Remember what I have told you."

8 The women ran quickly from the tomb. They were very frightened but also filled with great joy, and they rushed to give the disciples the angel's message.

9 And as they went, Jesus met them and greeted them. And they ran to him, grasped his feet, and worshiped him.

10 Then Jesus said to them, "Don't be afraid! Go tell my brothers to leave for Galilee, and they will see me there."

News Team 2
THOSE INVOLVED: Peter, John
SCRIPTURE: John 20:3-9

3 Peter and the other disciple started out for the tomb.

4 They were both running, but the other disciple outran Peter and reached the tomb first.

5 He stooped and looked in and saw the linen wrappings lying there, but he didn't go in.

6 Then Simon Peter arrived and went inside. He also noticed the linen wrappings lying there,

7 while the cloth that had covered Jesus' head was folded up and lying apart from the other wrappings.

8 Then the disciple who had reached the tomb first also went in, and he saw and believed—

9 for until then they still hadn't understood the Scriptures that said Jesus must rise from the dead.

EXTRA! EXTRA!
READ ALL ABOUT IT!
BREAKING NEWS!

News Team 3

THOSE INVOLVED: Some disciples, Jesus
SCRIPTURE: John 20:19-20

19 That Sunday evening the disciples were meeting behind locked doors because they were afraid of the Jewish leaders. Suddenly, Jesus was standing there among them! "Peace be with you," he said.

20 As he spoke, he showed them the wounds in his hands and his side. They were filled with joy when they saw the Lord!

News Team 4

THOSE INVOLVED: Disciples, Thomas, Jesus
SCRIPTURE: John 20:24-28

24 One of the twelve disciples, Thomas (nicknamed the Twin), was not with the others when Jesus came.

25 They told him, "We have seen the Lord!"

But he replied, "I won't believe it unless I see the nail wounds in his hands, put my fingers into them, and place my hand into the wound in his side."

26 Eight days later the disciples were together again, and this time Thomas was with them. The doors were locked; but suddenly, as before, Jesus was standing among them. "Peace be with you," he said.

27 Then he said to Thomas, "Put your finger here, and look at my hands. Put your hand into the wound in my side. Don't be faithless any longer. Believe!"

28 "My Lord and my God!" Thomas exclaimed.

Say: **Great job, everyone! We've heard the too-good news that** ★ *Jesus is alive!* **Hallelujah!**

LIFE APPLICATION

Jesus Is Alive Lilies

Say: **Many churches decorate with sweet-smelling Easter lilies on Easter. Some of you may even have Easter lilies in your homes. White lilies are great symbols for Easter. Their shape seems to trumpet the good news that** ★ *Jesus is alive!* **And their beautiful scent fills the room with the good news as well. Today we're going to make some beautiful paper Easter lilies that carry the message that** ★ *Jesus is alive!*

Lead kids to a craft area where you've set out scissors, glue sticks, cotton swabs, green and yellow markers, pencils, and copies of the "Jesus Is Alive Lily" handout (p. 83). It's best to lead kids by making your own lily step by step so they clearly see the folds involved.

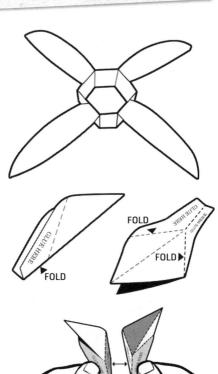

- ✓ Cut out the base with the leaves as well as the four lily petals.
- ✓ Color both sides of the leaves green.
- ✓ Bend the dotted lines back gently on the base piece. Glue the two ends together.
- ✓ Fold each of the four lily petals in half the long way so the dotted lines show.
- ✓ Fold the diagonal lines back and forth; then flatten again.
- ✓ Glue the two petals together at the bottom as indicated. Do the same with the other two petals.
- ✓ Paint the tips of three cotton swabs with a yellow marker. Sandwich them between the two halves of a lily so they protrude slightly.
- ✓ Pull the lily petals outward and roll the tips around a pencil.
- ✓ Curl the tips of the leaves lightly around a finger.
- ✓ Insert lily into center of base. If desired, glue lily to inner surface of base.

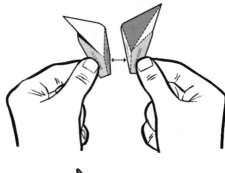

FOLD FOLD FOLD FOLD

GLUE HERE

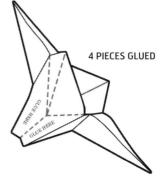

4 PIECES GLUED

GLUE HERE

All Together Now

Glue Here
Glue Here
Glue Here
Glue Here

Jesus Is Alive!

Jesus Is Alive!

Glue Here
Glue Here
Glue Here
Glue Here

Jesus Is Alive Lily

COMMITMENT

What's the Difference?

Gather kids in a circle with their Jesus Is Alive lilies in front of them. Place the Hula-Hoop in the center of the circle.

Say: **Today we've reported on and celebrated the fact that ★** *Jesus is alive!*

But now I have an important question for you, and it's not an easy one. You'll have to think about it for a bit before you stand in the Hula-Hoop to answer. Here we go.

Ask:

• **What difference does it make in your life that ★** *Jesus is alive?*

Say: **Here's a little help. You might want to start your answer with:** *It means that...***And please try not to copy another person's answer.**

When everyone who wants to has shared, say: **Thanks for your great thinking! Please remember it throughout this next week.**

CLOSING

Sing It Out!

Close with a favorite Easter praise song, such as "Easter Song," "He Is Lord," or others your kids know. You can play the song twice to encourage kids to sing along.

When your song is finished, shout, ★ *Jesus is alive!* and have kids shout it back to you.

Say: **Dear God, thank you for the precious gift of your Son. Thank you for giving our world the incredible, too-good news that ★** *Jesus is alive!* **In Jesus' name, amen.**

All Together Now

Into a Cloud

LESSON AIM

To help kids believe that ★ *Jesus gave us a job to do.*

OBJECTIVES

Kids will

✓ meet challenges to launch objects high in the air,

✓ use Gummy Bears, pretzels, and marshmallows to reenact Acts 1:1-11,

✓ make a "Witness for Jesus Quick Notes" craft, and

✓ participate in a witness cheer.

BIBLE BASIS

 John 20:19-20; Acts 1:1-11

The last two chapters of the Gospel of John and the first chapter of Acts focus on Jesus' post-resurrection appearances. He remained on earth for 40 days. He appeared human in various ways, such as eating (Acts 1:4). Even so, he also came and went in nonhuman ways, such as appearing and disappearing at will. He did many other things to prove to the disciples that he was alive. He kept on teaching about the kingdom of God, affirmed in the Emmaus account of Luke 24:13-31.

These facts about Jesus also teach a few things about the disciples. Even after Jesus' death and resurrection, they were a confused bunch, struggling to understand what Jesus' victory over death meant and how it would affect their immediate

You'll need...

☐ balloons*

☐ plastic garbage bag

☐ paper lunch bag containing 1 SuperBall per child

☐ antiseptic hand sanitizer

☐ Gummy Bears candies**

☐ thin pretzel sticks**

☐ large marshmallows**

☐ sandwich bags

☐ copies of the "Witness for Jesus Quick Notes" handout (p. 92)

☐ scissors

☐ pencils

☐ colorful paper clips

☐ hole punch

* Warning. Choking hazard— Children under 8 years old can choke or suffocate on uninflated or broken balloons. Adult supervision required. Keep uninflated balloons from children. Discard broken balloons at once. Balloons may contain latex.

** Always check for allergies before serving snacks.

future. I can relate to them, can't you? It's as if they were students in a great cosmic classroom, saying, "But—wait, I don't get it" and "Tell me more."

It seems that as the disciples who'd supported Jesus stayed in a locked room, out of sight of the Jews who'd killed Jesus, the risen Jesus came and went, teaching and encouraging them.

Isn't this how God works with us today, unfolding his plan little by little, meeting with us as we wait on him in prayer and meditation on his Word?

I wish the Bible gave us more detail on this largely mysterious period in Jesus' life. I would like to have been a mouse in the corner when Jesus taught his disciples as they huddled in their locked room. My hunger to know more about this fairly silent period of Jesus' life makes me feel like the disciples—*Tell me more!* It's easy to conjure a dozen questions about what went on while Jesus was coming and going, teaching and encouraging, but there's more to be gained by sticking to the obvious conclusions we can draw from what we learn at the end of John and in these opening 11 verses of Acts.

First, Jesus gave plenty of indisputable evidence that he was alive. Second, he prepared his disciples for the coming of the Holy Spirit. Third, he made it clear that his kingdom was not to be of this world, but would happen in God's own way, in God's own time. Fourth, he stated the Great Commission with the priority of beginning at home. Finally, he rose to heaven before many witnesses and with angelic affirmation.

And it's only the beginning of our adventures with the disciples and the early church!

📖 Psalm 62:5

In Acts 1:4, Jesus told the disciples to wait in Jerusalem until God sent the promised Holy Spirit. Waiting on God was not a new concept for the children of Israel. Throughout their history, the Israelites had often waited until the very last minute for God's redemption. Those who knew the heart of God, like the psalmists, found comfort and wisdom in waiting in his presence. Today, those of us who live with the pressure of instant communication can still find the greatest solace in turning off, tuning out, and simply waiting on God.

All Together Now

UNDERSTANDING YOUR KIDS

This lesson is filled with the supernatural acts of God as opposed to the fictionalized acts of a superhero. It's important to make that distinction crystal clear for your kids. Jesus took 40 days to make sure his disciples understood his transformation. He showed them his nailed-pierced hands and the wound in his side, and he ate with them. At the same time, he came and went in ways that defied normal human ability.

Kids easily cheer for feel-good superheroes. Now we're asking them to be *witnesses* for a real, live Jesus who appeared to as many as 500 people before he was taken to heaven (1 Corinthians 15:1-11).

Use this lesson to help your kids affirm their faith in Jesus' ascension into heaven and to equip them to be faithful witnesses of all that Jesus has done in their lives.

THE LESSON »

ATTENTION GRABBER

Higher, Higher, Higher!

Give kids a warm greeting. Let early arrivers help you inflate balloons. You'll need one balloon for each child plus a few extra in case some pop.

Say: **Today my challenge for you is to launch things high into the air. The first thing to launch is yourselves. Let's see who can jump the highest. Jump for the sky with one hand stretched in the air, and I'll use my keen eye to see who makes it the highest!**

Let kids jump for a few seconds before you proclaim the highest jumper. Then say: **Our second challenge involves balloons. You can bounce, bat, serve, or otherwise launch balloons into the air any way you can think of. Let's cheer each other on as our balloons go higher and higher!**

Bounce balloons to everyone. Keep kids cheering as their balloon-bopping skills grow and balloons go higher and higher into the air. Call time after a couple of minutes and collect the balloons in a plastic garbage bag.

Guide kids to a hard surface and say: **Here comes the final and most exciting challenge!**

Hold up the paper lunch bag containing SuperBalls and say: **This simple, inconspicuous bag contains a small quantity of one of the most amazing launchable items known to humankind. Once you tell me what my bag contains, I'll share them with you for our highest-in-the-sky launches yet!**

When someone guesses, toss a ball to each child.

Say: **Your job is to bounce your SuperBall as high as you can. Keep track of your own ball, and then bring it back and try to bounce it higher!**

After lots of bouncing fun, collect the balls, gather kids in a circle in your classroom, and say: **You've done a great job of launching things into the air today. Our Bible story is about something, or someone, who launched into the air and clear out of sight! You may need to buckle yourselves in for this one. It's going to be an amazing ride.**

Teacher Tip

Plan to teach this part of the lesson outside or in a high-ceilinged room.

BIBLE EXPLORATION

....

Into a Cloud (John 20:19-20; Acts 1:1-11)

Gather kids in a story circle. Make sure everyone has a copy of the Bible in an easy-to-understand translation.

Say: **Today's Bible passage is short, but full of interesting stuff! Let's begin by reading it aloud together. I'll read the first verse and then ask for volunteers to read each of the next verses.**

Read John 20:19 and then ask willing children to read John 20:20 and each verse of Acts 1:1-11.

After you've read through the passage as a class, gather the kids around a table but ask them not to sit down. Pass around a bottle of hand sanitizer and make sure each child uses it.

Say: **Today you're going to help me bring this Bible story alive with some extra-special props. I need to tell you before I hand them out that these props are not for eating—they're for telling!**

Give a Gummy Bear candy to each child. You'll need to hand out at least 16 Gummy Bear candies, so you may need to give some children two. Next, hand out several pretzel sticks to each child.

Say: **Now you're equipped to help me tell the first part of the story. Listen carefully so you can figure out what to do.**

For the first few days after Jesus rose from the dead, Jesus' disciples stayed in a locked room together. It may have been the same "upper room" where Jesus celebrated the Last Supper with his disciples. I wonder if you have supplies to make the outline of a room.

Give kids a few moments to outline a room with their pretzel sticks. Then say: **The people who stayed in the room probably included the *eleven* disciples plus *a few* women who followed Jesus and went to his tomb. Place these people in the room.**

They kept the room locked because they were afraid that the Jews and the Romans who had killed Jesus might come after them. Boy, were they surprised when Jesus came and stood in their midst, even though the doors were still locked!

If the children have already placed all their Gummy Bears in the room, add one of your own. Say: **Jesus said, "Peace be with you!"**

The disciples were filled with joy! If they had been Gummy Bear disciples, they might have even jumped for joy!

Give kids a moment to jump their Gummy Bear candies up and down. Then say: **One time when Jesus was eating with** his disciples, he told them (wiggle the Jesus figure a bit as you speak): **"Do not leave Jerusalem until, in just a few days, the Father sends you the Holy Spirit."**

Another time the disciples were with Jesus on a mountainside.

Carefully spill most of your bag of marshmallows on the table and say: **We need a mountain!**

Save a few marshmallows in the bag for the cloud that will enfold Jesus.

Say: **One of the disciples had this question for Jesus: "Will you take over Israel and make this your kingdom now?"**

The disciples were still wondering if he was going to be a king on earth.

Jesus answered, "The Father alone sets those dates and times and they're not for you to know. But soon you'll receive power from the Holy Spirit. Then you will be my witnesses, first right here in Jerusalem, then in all Judea, then a little farther out in Samaria, and then to the very ends of the earth!"

After Jesus said this, he rose into the air (raise your Gummy Bear candy into the air) **where a cloud covered him.**

With your other hand, spill the rest of the marshmallows onto the table and point to them so the children will use them to form a cloud. After the marshmallow cloud hides "Jesus," slide your Gummy Bear candy out of sight and finish the story.

The disciples kept looking up into the sky, but they couldn't see Jesus anymore. Have your Gummy Bears look up into the sky.

Continue in a hushed voice, and say: **Finally, two men clothed in dazzling white appeared among them and said, "Men of Galilee, why are you standing here staring into heaven? Jesus has been taken from you into heaven, but someday he will return from heaven in the same way you saw him go!"**

★*Jesus gave us a job to do!* **Thank you for doing a tremendous job helping me tell this Bible story! Give yourselves a great big cheer. Woohoo!**

Now, it's plain to see that we have a table full of treats here. Good thing I have a plan for sharing them!

Hand out sandwich bags and say: **We'll share the treats in rounds. On each round, everyone can pick up two treats from the table and put them into your sandwich bag.**

All Together Now

Find out which child's birthday is closest to Christmas. Have that child put two treats from the table in a sandwich bag; then proceed around the circle. After kids have collected their treats, let them eat one or two things from their bags.

Settle the kids in a circle and ask:

• **If you could ask one question of Jesus before he went to heaven, what would it be?**

• **Suppose you could have been in that locked room the first time Jesus appeared to his disciples. What do you think it would have been like to see, or witness, Jesus alive again?**

• **What do you think it means to be a witness?**

• **How do you feel about being Jesus' witness in your own town today?**

LIFE APPLICATION

Be My Witnesses

Ask:

• **Describe what a witness in a courtroom does.**

• **To be a witness for Jesus, what would you say or do?**

Explain how sometimes in a courtroom, lawyers call character witnesses. Character witnesses can say that they've known a person a long time, tell whether the person is someone who helps others, or say if the person is a faithful, trustworthy friend who always does the right thing. Say: **I have something that'll prepare each of you to be a character witness for Jesus. Let's form groups of three to work on these together.**

Set out scissors, pencils, colorful paper clips, a hole punch, and copies of the "Witness for Jesus Quick Notes" handout (p. 92). Kids can read the simple instructions on the handout.

Circulate among the groups as they work together to answer the questions on the handout.

Say: **Save two or three of the questions to work on with your family at home. Then your entire family will be ready to be witnesses for Jesus. ★**_Jesus gave us a job to do,_ **and that job is to be his witnesses!**

Witness for Jesus
Quick Notes

Cut out the three pages below, and then work with friends to discuss and write in answers to the questions. When you're done, stack the three pages, punch a hole through the circle on the first page and slip on a paper clip. You're all ready to be a witness for Jesus!

✓ What is your favorite Bible verse about Jesus?

✓ What's the best thing about knowing Jesus?

✓ How is Jesus different from friends on earth?

✓ How has Jesus been a friend to you?

✓ How did you get to know Jesus?

✓ When has Jesus answered your prayers?

Witness
for
Jesus

NAME

COMMITMENT

. . . .

Witnessing Role-Plays

Form a circle, but ask kids to stay near the kids they just worked with.

Ask:

• **What kinds of questions have people asked you about being a Christian?**

• **What do you think it mean to be a witness for Jesus?**

Say: **Since** ★ *Jesus gave us a job to do*, **let's practice what Jesus wanted us to do. In your groups, think of two different situations when you might have a chance to be a witness about your faith in Jesus. Here's a time I got that chance.** Be ready with a personal example.

After a couple of minutes, have volunteer kids from each group describe the situations they came up with. After each group offers a situation, ask the entire group:

• **If you were in this situation, what would be one way you could be a good character witness for Jesus?**

Keep going until all groups have presented their challenges and responded to the question. Thank kids for their great ideas.

Say: **Now you'll be ready to be a witness for your faith in Jesus!**

CLOSING

. . . .

A Closing Cheer

Say: **During this time together, we've been learning that** ★ *Jesus gave us a job to do*. **That job is to be witnesses for Jesus and to share his love with other people in our lives. Let's close with a cheer to help us remember everything we've learned. I'll say a line of the cheer, and then you repeat it after me. Ready...cheer!**

Jesus is my Savior
And my closest friend.
He gave his life for all our sins;
In three days rose again.
He stayed on earth for 40 days
To teach and help his friends.
He rose to heaven and will come back
But only God knows when!

Have kids stand in a circle and hold hands. Say: **Dear God, thank you for giving us the opportunity to be witnesses for Jesus. Thank you for entrusting us with the very important job of sharing Jesus' love and character with our friends. Please help us remember that when Jesus rose from the dead and went to heaven,** ★ *he gave us an important job to do.* **And help us do that job well! In Jesus' name, amen.**

Close with cheers, encourage kids to have a great week, and invite them back to the next lesson.

All Together Now

Here Comes the Holy Spirit

LESSON AIM

To help kids see how ★ *the Holy Spirit brings God's power.*

OBJECTIVES

Kids will

✓ play a Tug of War game that suddenly gets a big boost of power,

✓ recreate the scene at Pentecost with an interactive story,

✓ make a "Pentecost in Art" craft, and

✓ commit to being open to the Holy Spirit's power in their lives.

BIBLE BASIS

 Acts 2:1-41

You're probably familiar with the song "O Little Town of Bethlehem." Maybe we should think in terms of "O Little Place Called Israel." In Jesus' time Israel was not more than 120 miles long by 40 miles wide. Yet, as the chosen people of God, its people believed in their destiny of freedom and even dominance in the world. In reality, though, the Israelites were subjected to the Babylonian, Persian, Greek, and Roman Empires. Even moments before his ascension into heaven, Jesus' disciples were asking whether that would be the moment when Jesus would take earthly power.

You'll need...

☐ masking tape

☐ clothesline or other long, heavy rope

☐ teenage or adult volunteers to add power to your Tug of War game

☐ whistle

☐ two large box fans

☐ extension cords as needed

☐ jar candles

☐ lighter

☐ scissors

☐ markers

☐ glue sticks

☐ copies of the "Pentecost in Art" handout (p. 102)

The feast of Pentecost comes. Jerusalem is once again overcrowded with pilgrims from all over the world. As Jesus commanded, his followers gathered in Jerusalem, waiting for the Holy Spirit promised by Jesus. Acts 1:15 tells us there were about 120 of these followers. Here's a new title for our song: "O Little Group of Followers." The story of Jesus lies on the shoulders of these few.

Then the Holy Spirit of God comes upon the group with the sound of a wind so great that it draws crowds to the house where the disciples were staying. Tongues of fire appear to sit on the heads of the waiting ones. *Now,* you impatient disciples, *now* you unknowing, unseeing sons and daughters of Israel, *now is your time!*

From Israel has been born the Son of David, the Son of God, who has risen from death and sits at the right hand of God. And though the leaders of Israel rejected Jesus, God sent the unlearned men and women of Galilee who did follow him to spill out of the house, speaking the good news of his life and death and resurrection so that the people in the burgeoning crowd could hear it in their own languages. *Now, Israel, now!*

Peter's voice booms forth, taking the crowd captive. This is no bumbling Peter, doing the right thing one moment and the wrong thing the next. This spirit-filled Peter shreds the hearts of those who have not yet wrapped themselves in the shredded flesh of the Savior. And by the very power of God, the 120 become the 3,000.

The church is born. Within a lifetime it will spread to the known world by the very power of God.

The very power of God, the Holy Spirit of God, is with us today. Those who believe in Jesus live in openness to the Spirit's power. Sometimes it is a still, small voice. Sometimes it's a roaring, mighty wind.

On the day of Pentecost, the Spirit came in great power to a large group of people. As we venture on with the early church, we'll see the Spirit manifest itself through a smaller group of people and even one person to great effect.

God did not come in power to Israel in the way the Jews expected. God rarely comes in power in our lives according to our best laid plans. One of the very earliest lessons I wrote was titled "God Surprises Us." That's still a core part of my thinking and my experience with God. We have our plans—God has better ones!

Open yourself daily to the magnificent Spirit of God. Be aware of God's presence and power. Obey the many commands throughout Scripture to wait patiently on the Lord. Live in expectation.

God never fails to surprise us!

All Together Now

📖 **Joel 2:28-32**

An unusual outpouring of God's Spirit had long been predicted by the prophet Joel. And the Jews knew their Scriptures! In Peter's Pentecost sermon, he did a marvelous, God-empowered job of opening the Scriptures the crowds in Jerusalem had long known and applying them to Jesus.

The Holy Spirit worked not only in Peter's preaching, but also in quickening the hearts of the listeners. Joel's words suddenly took on new urgency, new clarity.

We who are witnesses for Jesus sometimes mistakenly think that the burden of persuasion lies on us. Not so! The Holy Spirit also works in the hearts and minds of those who are willing to listen.

UNDERSTANDING YOUR KIDS

Kids know what it's like to feel small and helpless. They answer to everybody—parents, teachers, coaches, instructors in music, gymnastics, or whatever hobbies they follow. Those hobbies may even be "chosen" for them.

Yet Jesus loved and welcomed children and held them up as examples of what God's kingdom is like. The wisdom that pours from a child's mouth often puts adults to shame.

It's great for kids to know they, too, can be difference-makers in this world when they listen to God, heed his voice, and open themselves to the workings of his power.

THE LESSON »

ATTENTION GRABBER

Power Up Tug of War

Welcome kids warmly and have them begin forming teams with equal strength for a game of Tug of War. It's best for you to assign teams rather than going through the last-to-be chosen process for kids who are less strong than others.

When you have two teams, stick a three-foot masking tape line on the floor between them. Fold a heavy clothesline in half. Mark the middle point with a piece of masking tape. Place the middle point on the masking tape line on the floor and place your foot on it. Have the teams line up for Tug of War starting 5 feet back from the middle line, with smaller players in front and larger players in back. Toss each team its half of the clothesline.

Say: **Straighten your rope and stand over it. The first person in line will stand on one side of the rope, the second person will stand on the other side, and so on. When you have yourselves arranged, pick up the rope.**

When I remove my foot, pull *gently* **on the rope, just to pick up the slack. I repeat:** *gently.*

Pause for kids to repeat *gently.* Remove your foot, and then give a sequence of commands in which you tell kids to pull a little harder, a little harder, a little harder, and then really hard. When one team drags the other past the masking tape line, blow the whistle, and say:

Well done, everyone! Whew—that was a lot of work. Let's take a minute for a few deep breaths.

Lead kids in a few slow, deep breaths, and then ask:

• **What you would think about adding some power to our teams?**

Go to the door and admit the volunteers you've invited to add power to your teams. Encourage the volunteers to playfully show their muscles as they join the teams.

Say: **Let's play again!**

Lead the game as you did before. As the volunteers leave the room, have everyone give them a round of applause for adding their power to the game. Then gather the kids in a discussion circle.

• **How was playing the game the second time different from the first time?**

• **Can you tell about a time when you needed a big boost of power like we got in our game today?**

Say: **Today we're going to discover how ★ *the Holy Spirit***

Prep Box

Ask an added source of power for your Tug of War game to join you shortly after your lesson begins. It might be two strong men from your congregation or a group of teenagers—anyone who would add significant power to the game. Arrange to play this game in a large, open room or outside.

All Together Now

brings God's power. **Are you ready to travel back in time to right after Jesus rose into heaven? It's going to be quite a trip! Let's go!**

BIBLE EXPLORATION

Holy Spirit Power! (Acts 2:1-41)

Say: **Jesus' disciples are waiting in Jerusalem, just as Jesus told them to do before he rose into heaven. They may even be in the same upper room where they shared the Last Supper. We're going to join them, but we'll have to be careful as we travel through the streets of Jerusalem to get there.**

Remember, Jesus' followers have remained in hiding most of the time because the same people who killed Jesus may come after them. I checked out what I think is a safe route to the upper room earlier this morning, but you never can tell where spies might pop up. So stick close to me, move quickly and quietly, and don't go around any corners until I give you the all-clear signal. Got it?

Lead kids in an exciting, circuitous dash around halls of your church. Have them hug the walls, remain as much out of sight as possible, and move with great stealth until you arrive at your designated upper room location. Gather kids in a circle on the floor, and say: **Good job making it here without attracting the attention of any spies! I don't think we've put any of Jesus' followers in danger. Whew! Now let's find out what happens.**

Hand a copy of an easy-to-read version of the Bible opened to Acts chapter 2 to a child volunteer who's a confident reader. Ask your reader to read the first three verses, pausing after each verse.

After verse 1 say: **Pentecost was another big feast time in Jerusalem when the city was filled with pilgrims from far and wide. God certainly knows how to time things!**

After verse 2, ask two children to turn your box fans on medium.

Say: **There was no real storm, just a *sound* like a roaring, mighty wind. And it was only in the house where the disciples where staying! Here's something interesting to remember: In Hebrew, the words for *spirit* and *wind* are the same word—*ruach*. So the *wind* and God's Holy *Spirit* entered the house at the same time!**

Prep Box

Find a special area in your church to teach this Bible story. It might be a balcony, a large landing on stairs, a chapel, or any place you can find that's set apart and gives a feeling of privacy. Place two large box fans in this area along with a row of jar candles on a table.

After verse 3, light the row of jar candles. You may need to turn the box fans to low or off to do so.

Say: **At special times, God used fire to represent his presence. God spoke to Moses from the bush that burned but never burned up. Priests kept seven lamps lit on the big golden candlestick in the Tabernacle and the Temple. Now God brought that power right to Jesus' followers!**

Hold your hands above your head and move your fingers like flames of fire.

Pause as kids do this, and then say: **That same power of the Holy Spirit can dwell in you!**

Have your reader read verses four through eight uninterrupted. Then say: **The noise from the Spirit wind was so great that crowds began gathering outside the house to see what was going on. Isn't that interesting—the sound of a great windstorm coming from just one house!**

But when curious people got to the house, they heard something even more bewildering! Jesus' disciples poured out of the house proclaiming the good news about Jesus. Although people in the crowd came from many different countries, they each heard the good news in their own language!

I wonder if any of you knows how to speak a different language? When I count to three, we'll all say *Jesus loves you!* If you know a different language, say *Jesus loves you* in a different language. If English is the only language you know, go ahead and say it in English.

Ready? One, two, three.

Jesus loves you!

Wow! That's a little how it sounded to the crowd that gathered around the house where the disciples were staying. Everyone was amazed!

Then Peter stepped forward to address the crowd. He was full of the power of the Holy Spirit. He explained that Jesus was the Christ, the Son of God, the Messiah God had promised hundreds of years before. Peter told everyone to repent of their sins and to be baptized in the name of Jesus; then they too could receive the Holy Spirit.

After Peter's sermon, the number of Jesus' followers increased from 120 to 3,000.

Let's lift our hands to heaven as a way of saying thank you that ★ *the Holy Spirit brings God's power!*

Teacher Tip

If you're comfortable in another language, say, "Jesus loves you" in that language.

100

All Together Now

Turn off the fans and gather the kids in a discussion circle. Ask:

• **How were the disciples changed when God filled them with the power of the Holy Spirit?**

• **How is that like the way things changed when you got extra power for our Tug of War teams? How is it different?**

• **How do we know the Holy Spirit is still with us today?**

Say: **God's Holy Spirit is with people who put their faith in Jesus. Jesus explained that he went back to heaven so God could send the Holy Spirit to us. When we open our hearts to listen to the Holy Spirit and do his will, we never know when wonderful things will happen through his power.** ★ *The Holy Spirit brings God's power!*

Extinguish the candles, and then lead the group back to your meeting area.

LIFE APPLICATION

Pentecost in Art

Lead kids to your craft area where you've laid out the markers, scissors, glue sticks, and the "Pentecost in Art" handouts (p. 102).

Simple instructions for completing the piece are printed on the handout. Encourage kids to think of the Holy Spirit coming at Pentecost as they color the sections that represent the wind and fire of the Holy Spirit.

As kids are creating, ask:

• **Explain why you chose certain colors to represent the wind of the Spirit.**

• **How does what we've learned today make you think of the Holy Spirit in a different way?**

Invite kids who finish first to begin to clean up the craft area. When everyone is done, invite kids to form a discussion circle with their art projects in the center.

Say: ★ *The Holy Spirit brings God's power.* **The writer of Acts was a man named Luke. He described the wonder of that day as best he could in human terms. And you've used art to describe the way you imagine that day.**

Now let's see what difference the coming of the Holy Spirit can mean in our lives from day to day.

Prep Box

Make a finished model of the "Pentecost in Art" handout (p. 102) so kids have an idea of what the finished three-dimensional piece looks like.

Teacher Tip

Small fingers may need help folding and gluing the tabs to the back of the card. As older kids finish, encourage them to help younger ones.

Pentecost in Art

At Pentecost, the Holy Spirit came first in wind and then in tongues of fire. Cut out the card below, fold it in half, and color the windstorm. Color the row of flames and then cut them out, just to the point where the flames connect to the horizontal strip. Place the flames in front of the card. Fold the tabs back on each side and glue them to the back of the front of the card.

THE HOLY SPIRIT BRINGS GOD'S POWER

COMMITMENT

The Power to Speak

Ask:

• **Describe how you think the disciples were different after they received the power of the Holy Spirit.**

• **In what ways can you be witnesses, like the disciples were, for Jesus?**

Say: **Sometimes the Holy Spirit comes in great power upon a group of people, like in today's Bible passage. Sometimes the Holy Spirit comes to us in quiet ways when we're singing about Jesus or praying. Sometimes the Holy Spirit nudges us to do or say something kind. And sometimes the Holy Spirit gives us the power to turn away from anger and respond the way Jesus would respond.**

Tell the kids about a time the Holy Spirit helped you give a Jesus-like response or prompted you to be kind in a way that made a difference in another person's life. Then encourage kids to share their own experiences of responding to God's gentle promptings in their own lives.

Say: **There are times when we are witnesses for Jesus by speaking about him and times when we are his witnesses by acting like him. ★ *The Holy Spirit brings God's power* into our lives to do all of those things. Turn to a friend and discuss one way you'll take time to listen to God's Holy Spirit this week.**

After kids have had a few moments for discussion, encourage several to share their ideas.

CLOSING

Motion Prayer

Ask kids to stand with you in a circle to begin this open-eyed motion prayer. Tell kids to follow your motions.

1. Cross your hands over your heart.

Say: **Let's pray. Heavenly Father, we worship you. We thank you for sending the ★ *Holy Spirit to bring your power.***

2. Open your hands near your heart.

Say: **We open our hearts to your love and grace.**

3. Put your hands to your ears.

Say: **Help us take time to listen to your guiding voice,**

4. Stretch your arms straight in front of you.

Say: **And to be witnesses for Jesus through our actions and our words.**

5. Drop your arms to your sides.

Say: **In Jesus' name, amen.**

Face-Off With the Sanhedrin

You'll need...

- ☐ copy of the "Role-Plays" handout (p. 109)
- ☐ paper lunch bags
- ☐ copies of the "Peter Puppet Add-Ons" handout (p. 113)
- ☐ markers
- ☐ scissors
- ☐ glue sticks

LESSON AIM

To help kids realize that ★ *God helps us speak the truth boldly.*

OBJECTIVES

Kids will

✓ role-play situations in which kids get in trouble without doing anything wrong,

✓ participate in a cue and response story about Peter and John healing a man and appearing before the Sanhedrin, and

✓ make a Peter paper-bag puppet.

BIBLE BASIS

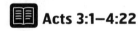 **Acts 3:1–4:22**

After the coming of the Holy Spirit at Pentecost, the disciples who'd previously holed up in a locked room out of fear had no qualms about moving freely around Jerusalem. Not only that, they returned to their old practices of going to the Temple for the main hours of prayer—in this case, 3:00 in the afternoon.

A beggar who from birth had not been able to walk wisely had himself placed near the Beautiful Gate of the Temple, probably the gate that separated the Court of the Gentiles from the Court of the Women. All Jews were expected to be merciful to the poor, and what better time to remind them of this than when they were on their way into the Temple to pray! This particular beggar had probably become part of the landscape to many of the Temple worshippers, but on this day he caught Peter's eye.

Peter and John commanded the beggar, "Look at us!" The man must have had his money receptacle eagerly at the ready, but a look at the apostles would have told him that they were men of no great monetary means. Can you imagine the jaw-dropping effect of these great words of Peter's? "I don't have any silver or gold for you. But I'll give you what I have. In the name of Jesus Christ the Nazarene, get up and walk!"

A strong right hand from the big fisherman helped the man to his feet, and instantly his feet and ankles grew strong. The beggar couldn't contain his joy! He went leaping about on those newly strengthened legs for all to see. The awestruck crowd recognized the formerly disabled beggar and wondered at the sight. Made wise by the Holy Spirit, Peter called out to the crowd and named the source of the healing power to be Jesus Christ of Nazareth. Before he finished preaching, 2,000 more had joined the church.

It didn't take long for the Temple guards to lock up Peter and John. The two men appeared before the Sanhedrin, the very body that condemned Jesus, the next day. If the elders of Israel thought they could intimidate our two brave disciples, they were dead wrong. Rather, Peter ended up giving the Sanhedrin a scalding rebuke.

The frustrated Jewish leaders could do nothing, for there with Peter and John stood the healed man—the evidence of Jesus' healing power. The evidence of the power of the Holy Spirit.

The elders of Israel wondered at Peter and John's boldness, knowing that they were simple Galilean fishermen, not men trained in matters of the law. When they ordered the disciples to speak no more of Jesus, the power and eloquence of Peter's response reached a new height: *Do you think God wants us to obey you rather than him?*

What a goosebumps story! What a fire-in-the-heart moment! And how blessed to know that the same Holy Spirit who inspired Peter and John in the face of the Sanhedrin can work within us 2,000 years later!

📖 Psalm 118

The key tie-in from this Psalm is verse 22: *The stone that the builders rejected has now become the cornerstone.* Jesus quoted it

All Together Now

(Matthew 21:42), and now Peter repeats it to the Sanhedrin.

But look at everything else there is to dip into in this wonderful psalm! Read verses 6-9 and think of Peter's and John's attitudes as they stood before the frowning faces of the very body that condemned Jesus. Wow. Read through the entire psalm and identify how many phrases have become the basis of familiar worship songs.

This rich passage of Scripture is the perfect center for your quiet time with God this week.

UNDERSTANDING YOUR KIDS

A child might compare Peter and John's experience before the Sanhedrin to the dreaded trip to the principal's office. Or the reckoning moment with any person of authority whom they've innocently crossed before. They understand stammering lips, sweaty palms, a racing heart, and panic running just below the surface.

What a comfort to them to learn that God won't abandon them in the most intimidating situations. As young pilgrims in their journey with Jesus, the Spirit of God goes before them, behind them, beside them, and dwells within them.

Use this lesson to help kids believe that God's Spirit can empower them ★ *to speak the truth boldly.*

THE LESSON >>

ATTENTION GRABBER
· ·

Caught Doing Good

Say: **Let's begin today by role-playing three situations. It'll be up to you to figure out how the three situations connect.**

Help kids form three groups. (It's fine if a group has as few as two kids.) Hand each group one of the role-plays from the "Role-Plays" handout (p. 109). Give kids a few minutes to prepare, and then have them present their role-plays to the group.

Have the group applaud each small group after its role-play presentation. Then say:

What's similar about all those role-plays? Take a minute to talk with your group before you answer.

Let children discuss this until they come up with the idea that in each of the role-plays, a character got into trouble for doing something good.

Say: **It's a pretty confusing feeling to be "caught" for doing something good, isn't it? When that happens, we don't automatically say,** *Stop! You need to understand that I was doing the right thing. I was trying to be like Jesus!*

In today's Bible passage we'll see how two of Jesus' disciples got caught for doing something very good. And when they did, they got put in a scary situation. But even in that scary situation, ★ *God helped them speak the truth boldly.* **Let's see what we can discover to help us speak the truth boldly.**

BIBLE EXPLORATION
· ·

Peter and John Speak the Truth Boldly
(Acts 3:1–4:22)

Say: **When the Holy Spirit came at Pentecost, the disciples stopped hiding. They moved out into the streets and started telling everyone about Jesus. Not only did they tell people about Jesus, they did some of the same kinds of miracles that Jesus did when he was on earth. For example, one day...**

Wait a minute—it's time to get you involved! Explain to kids that you're going to repeat a few important words as the story continues. Tell kids each time you say one of the important words,

All Together Now

Role-Plays

- Child 1 is having trouble working out a math problem.
- Child 2 turns around to explain the problem to Child 1.
- Teacher is tired of all the extra talking in class and says: *Everyone who's talking raise your hand! You will stay in from recess and do extra math work today.*

- Child 1 visits a local store with friends.
- Child 1's friends are stealing, but Child 1 tries to persuade them to put the stolen things back.
- Child 1 is held with friends at store until police arrive and then taken home by police who explain that while Child 1 was innocent, friends shoplifted.
- Parent of Child 1 is disappointed and angry with Child 1.

- Child 1 invites Child 2 over to play.
- Child 2 grabs a ball and starts throwing it around the dining room.
- Child 1 urges Child 2 to take the ball outside, and heads out the back door.
- Child 2 again throws the ball inside, accidentally hitting Child 1's elderly grandmother in the head and causing her to cry.
- Child 1 rushes to crying grandmother and tries to comfort her. Child 1 feels terrible.
- Parent scolds Child 1 and sends Child 2 home.

they'll give a certain response. Take a moment to teach kids the cues and responses. Each time you teach a response, model it and have kids do it with you. Say:

- ✓ **Whenever I say "Temple," use your arms to make a roof over your head.**
- ✓ **Whenever I say "beggar," hold out your hands and say, "Help the poor!"**
- ✓ **Whenever I say "Peter" or "Peter and John," pump your fist and say "Yes!"**
- ✓ **Whenever I say "Jewish leaders," pretend to stroke your beard and say "Hmm."**
- ✓ **Whenever I say "Jesus," point a finger in the air, stand, and say, "Christ the Lord!"**

Call out the cue words in random order to make sure the kids have the responses down. Rehearse until you're satisfied that the kids are confident with their responses.

In the story below, each of the cue words is italicized for your convenience. Emphasize the cue words, pausing to let children respond with vigor.

Say: **One day, *Peter and John* went up to the *Temple* to pray at the time for afternoon prayers. Inside the *Temple*, beside the Beautiful Gate, sat a crippled *beggar*. The *beggar* sat in the same spot every day, hoping that people who were on their way to pray would remember that God had commanded them to be merciful to the poor.**

This *beggar* caught the attention of *Peter and John*. He looked at them hopefully, thinking they would give him money. But *Peter and John* looked closely at the *beggar* and commanded him, "Look at us." *Peter* looked the *beggar* right in the eye and said, "I don't have any silver or gold. But what I do have, I'll give you. In the name of *Jesus*, get up and walk!"

The *beggar* looked shocked. But when *Peter* held out his strong right hand, the *beggar* took it and stood up. All at once the *beggar's* feet and ankles grew strong. He was so excited that he started jumping and leaping all over the *Temple*!

Interrupt the story to explain that the children need to use a new response for the beggar. The new response is to jump out of chairs and shout "Woo-hoo!" Practice this response a few times, and then proceed with the story, saying:

All Together Now

The *beggar* couldn't stop himself from jumping and leaping and praising God all over the *Temple*! The other worshippers in the *Temple* recognized that the man who was jumping and leaping and praising God was the same *beggar* who could not walk, who had sat by the Beautiful Gate of the *Temple* for years and years. Their hearts were filled with wonder!

Peter jumped up onto one of the porches of the *Temple* to speak to the crowd. "Faith in the name of Jesus healed this man," he declared. Before *Peter* finished preaching, 2,000 more people believed in *Jesus*!

Seeing what was going on, the *Jewish leaders* sent men to arrest *Peter and John* and throw them in jail overnight. The next day *Peter and John* had to appear before the *Jewish leaders*. Remember, this was the same group of men who had arrested and condemned *Jesus*!

But do you think *Peter and John* were afraid? Not at all. They stood boldly before the *Jewish leaders* and proclaimed that they had healed the *beggar* in the name of *Jesus*. They said, "There is salvation in no one else! God has given no other name under heaven by which we must be saved."

The *Jewish leaders* mumbled and grumbled. They couldn't argue with *Peter and John*, because the healed *beggar* was standing right beside them. So they strictly ordered the disciples never again to teach in the name of *Jesus*.

But God helped *Peter and John* speak the truth boldly.

"Who are we to obey," *Peter* asked, "God or you? We can't help telling about the things we have seen and heard!"

The *Jewish leaders* could hardly believe how boldly *Peter and John* had spoken. They had expected the disciples to be afraid. But no! ★ *God helped* Peter and John *speak the truth boldly.*

The church grew and everyone praised God for the great miracle of the *beggar* being healed.

Join the kids in a big round of applause for the help they gave you in telling the Bible story. Then ask everyone to join you in a discussion circle.

Ask:

• **Why do you think Peter and John healed the beggar in the name of Jesus?**

• **How could Peter and John speak the truth about Jesus so bravely and boldly to the very men who had declared Jesus guilty?**

Say: ★ *God helps us speak the truth boldly!*
Ask:

• **When has God helped you speak the truth boldly?**

• **When is it most difficult to speak the truth about Jesus?**

• **How can the Holy Spirit help you speak the truth boldly?**

LIFE APPLICATION

Speak the Truth Boldly Puppets

Say: ★ *God helps us speak the truth boldly,* **and he certainly helped Peter and John in today's Bible passage. Now we're going to make a fun and simple paper-bag puppet of Peter as a reminder. I'll give you each a paper lunch bag and a handout of add-ons to turn your lunch bag into Peter.**

All you need to do is color in Peter's head and robe, cut them out, and glue them to the lunch bag. Presto! You'll have a Peter puppet!

Lead kids to the craft area where you've set out markers, scissors, glue sticks, paper lunch bags, and copies of the "Peter Puppet Add-Ons" handout (p. 113). This is a simple project. Kids just need to glue the head add-on to the folded bottom of the bag and the robe to the body of the bag.

As kids finish, encourage them to clean up the craft area. Then invite them to bring their puppets and join you in a discussion circle.

COMMITMENT

Telling the Truth About Jesus

Have kids form pairs and take turns using their Peter puppets to tell today's Bible story from Peter's perspective. For instance, one partner might tell half the story, and the other partner might take over and tell the rest of the story.

After pairs have had time to tell the story, gather the group and say: ★ *God helps us speak the truth boldly,* **especially when it comes to telling others about Jesus.**

All Together Now

Peter Puppet Add-Ons

Color and cut out Peter's head and robe.
Glue the head to the folded bottom of a paper lunch bag.
Glue the robe to the body of the lunch bag, below the head.
Use your Peter puppet to tell today's Bible story from his point of view!

Ask:

• **How can you use your puppets and your Bible storytelling to tell others the truth about Jesus?**

Say: **I hope you and your Peter puppets will be busy telling others about Jesus this week, relying on God's help!**

CLOSING

Truth-Teller's Prayer

Gather kids in a circle for prayer.

Dear God, thank you for helping Peter and John speak the truth about Jesus boldly. Thank you for sending the Holy Spirit to help us speak the truth about Jesus. God, please give us sensitive hearts and ★ *help us speak the truth boldly,* telling others that Jesus Christ is Lord whenever you give us an opportunity. We pray this in Jesus' name, amen.

All Together Now

A Strange Meeting

LESSON AIM

To help kids understand that ★ *Jesus shows us the right path.*

OBJECTIVES

Kids will

✓ choose from two paths in hopes of finding a treat,

✓ hear Ananias tell of his dilemma,

✓ create a "Pathway Through the Bible" fold-out book, and

✓ commit to making loving choices.

BIBLE BASIS

 **Acts 9:1-19**

At first read, this description of Saul "breathing out murderous threats against the Lord's disciples" (TNIV) makes this zealous persecutor of Christians sound fearfully dragonlike, doesn't it? In describing Saul in Acts 8:3, Luke uses an especially strong word for *destroy*, one that is normally associated with being torn up by a wild animal. What could motivate such blood lust in a Pharisee, one who was wholly committed to following even the tiniest aspect of God's Law? Such actions could only have come from a heart filled with rage.

Scholars are divided as to whether Saul was a member of the Sanhedrin, the group who had been so enraged at Stephen's

You'll need...

- ☐ treats*
- ☐ bag of onions*
- ☐ masking tape
- ☐ volunteer to play the role of Ananias
- ☐ Bible-times costume
- ☐ copy of "Ananias' Script" (pp. 120-121)
- ☐ scissors
- ☐ glue sticks
- ☐ copies of the "Pathway Through the Bible" handout (p. 123)

* Always check for allergies before serving snacks.

testimony that they had him dragged out of the city and stoned. Stephen's mob-like death was clearly illegal according to Roman law. But Saul is named as a consenting witness to this awful event. Thus, even if Saul wasn't a member of the Sanhedrin, he was probably on the "fast track" to becoming part of it.

Those who rejected Jesus saw his "new covenant" as a blasphemy to be stomped out as quickly as possible. In doing so they became blinded to the raging hate that consumed them—hate that could not originate from a loving God. We can assume that some members of the Sanhedrin became extremely jealous of Jesus' popularity among the people. The Sanhedrin wrested what little power it could from the Roman authorities. When the upstart prophet from the backward territory of Galilee cut into that, it was unbearable for them. Saul himself had studied under the famed teacher Gamaliel. Was he, too, hanging onto pride?

Imagine the frustration of the Jewish leaders when Jesus' crucifixion failed to quell the fervor of his followers. With the coming of the Holy Spirit, the disciples preached boldly and the church grew quickly, far beyond the 120 Jesus left behind at his ascension. Saul went from door to door in Jerusalem, arresting and terrorizing followers of Jesus. This passage finds him with special permission to go to Damascus to do the same there.

It took a supernatural encounter with Jesus himself on the road to stop Saul. He had to be blinded before he could see—humbled, stumbling, dependent on others to find his way. And then Saul was at the mercy of Ananias, a man of great faith, to have his sight restored, to be welcomed into the fellowship of believers and instructed in the Way. The man with a vicious mission suddenly found himself not only confronted by Jesus, but also lost, blind, and dependent on the very people he'd systematically terrorized to help him find his way.

The faithful Ananias obediently healed and interacted with Saul, the archenemy of Christians. We know little of Ananias other than what we can derive from the context. He was obviously a leader of Christians in Damascus—possibly even one of Saul's first targets for arrest!

Compare Ananias' faith and acceptance of God's directions to your own. Could you have so quickly come to the aid of someone who was your archenemy? I question my own ability in that regard, sometimes fearful and unforgiving individual that I am.

What a challenge this passage presents to all Jesus-followers, to believe in his limitless power to change people!

All Together Now

📖 **Ezekiel 36:26-27**

The Israelites had a long history of turning away from God, suffering the consequences, turning away from God, suffering the consequences, and so on. By rejecting God's only Son, the Jews took their rebellion to a new level. Throughout his life, Jesus fulfilled prophecy after prophecy, but unseeing eyes and hearts of stone refused to acknowledge the long-predicted events that were playing before them. Saul was definitely without sight and hardhearted.

But God had plans for this persecutor of the church. Saul, also known as Paul, had just the right background to present the gospel to the Hellenistic world. Through Jesus' supernatural appearance and Paul's blinding and subsequent healing and welcome by the Christians at Damascus, God did indeed turn Paul's heart from a heart of stone to a heart of flesh and put a new spirit, the Holy Spirit, within him.

In the end, no one did more to spread the gospel outside of Israel than Paul, a native of what is now Turkey. But to get Paul there, God literally had to knock him down on his behind! Let's hope that God can get our attention without resorting to such drastic measures.

UNDERSTANDING YOUR KIDS

Can a bad guy be completely transformed into a good guy? Saul's transformation to Paul stretches the imagination, because it's no ordinary transformation—it's miraculous!

When kids have been persecuted by a bully in their own world, they may not be so easily persuaded to accept overtures of friendship. After all, it could be a trick that will come back to haunt them in the end.

As a rule, the younger the child, the more quick he or she is to forgive. As kids grow older and more sophisticated, their instincts tell them not to be so quick to trust someone with a history of hurting them.

Use this lesson to teach kids that Jesus can show even the less desirable characters in our lives the right path. It takes courageous Christians like Ananias to welcome such people and bring them along in the faith.

THE LESSON »

ATTENTION GRABBER

Treat Trackers

Greet kids warmly and explain that today's time together will begin with a great adventure.

Say: **When we head out the door together, we'll find a path marked in the hallway. If we follow the path correctly, it'll lead us to treats. But if we choose wrong, we'll end up with a bag of onions! Remember, other groups may be meeting, so we'll be quiet trackers. When we head out the door, let's stay together—no running ahead. If we find that there are decisions to make, we'll make them as a group.**

Assemble kids by the door before you depart. When you arrive at the fork in the path, have kids vote on which direction to go. If their decision causes the group to arrive at the bag of onions, have them retrace their steps to the fork in the path and then take the other fork. When they've claimed the treats, follow the path back to your meeting area.

Gather the kids in a circle. Allow them to enjoy the treats as you ask:

• **What happened when we made our choice at the fork?**

• **What would you feel if you *never* got a chance to go back to the fork that took us to the treat rather than the onions?**

• **Tell about a time you realized you were on the wrong path in life and decided to turn back and find a better direction.** (Be ready with an example of your own.)

Say: **Jesus doesn't get angry with us when we make a decision that puts us on a wrong path. But one of the great things about following Jesus is that ★ *Jesus shows us the right path.***

We might think we're doing the right thing, and then Jesus speaks to our heart and all of a sudden we realize we need to make a course correction. Sometimes our course correction is a little change in attitude, but other times it may be a great big turnaround.

That's what happened to the main person in today's Bible passage. In fact, his turnaround was so huge that he even got a new name! Let's plunge right in and find out what happened.

All Together Now

BIBLE EXPLORATION

A Strange Meeting (Acts 9:1-19)

Say: **We have a distinguished visitor today—a main person in today's Bible passage. I've invited him to join us because he can tell us about what happened like no one else can. I hope you'll receive him with great respect. He's come across the world, all the way from the city of Damascus to tell his story. Let's prepare a chair for him and give him a heartfelt welcome!**

Go to the door to admit your Ananias actor.

After Ananias exits, ask:

• **How did Jesus show Saul the right path?**

• **How did Jesus show Ananias the right path?**

• **Why was Ananias surprised by the path Jesus asked him to take?**

Prep Box

Choose an adult volunteer, preferably an older man, to play the role of Ananias. Give the person a copy of "Ananias' Script" (pp. 120-121) and a Bible-times costume. Have him wait outside the door of your meeting area until you invite him in.

Ananias' Script

*Enter the meeting area in Bible-times costume and
sit down with the children. Draw them
into the drama of your story.*

I'm so glad to see you, young followers of Jesus!

I've come to tell you how Jesus showed me the right path when
the famous Saul of Tarsus came to Damascus, my hometown.

Have you heard of Saul of Tarsus? Saul was a Pharisee, and one
of the greatest enemies of those who followed Jesus. In the city
of Jerusalem, he dragged our brothers and sisters in Jesus to
prison in chains and had them beaten.

Then came the day we got word that Saul was coming our way
with permission to arrest Christians and take them back to
Jerusalem in chains. All the way to Damascus—that's 135 miles!
And of course he would have to come on foot, or at best on
horseback, through hot desert lands. We prayed and trusted
God, not knowing what would happen to us.

So you can imagine my confusion when one day Jesus clearly
spoke to me and told me to go to the house where Saul was
staying. He explained that Saul was blind and that I was to heal
him.

"But, Lord," I protested, "I've heard many reports of the terrible
things Saul has done to the Christians in Jerusalem! And now he
is authorized to arrest anyone who calls on your name."

God assured me that going to heal Saul was the right thing to do,
that Saul would take his message to Gentiles and even to kings.

Oh, I struggled to understand all this. *What if it was a trick*, I thought. *What if Saul was just pretending to be blind and the minute I entered the room he arrested me?* But then I remembered that Jesus had spoken to me clearly and that ★ *Jesus shows us the right path*.

I started toward the house where Saul was staying, praying all the way. When I got there, the host led me into a room and for the first time I saw Saul of Tarsus. He didn't look as fearsome as I had imagined him. No...he looked broken and lost.

Praying that the Holy Spirit would be with me in a mighty way, I put my hands on the head of this man who was once my enemy and said, "Brother Saul, the Lord Jesus, who appeared to you on the road, has sent me so that you can see again and be filled with the Holy Spirit."

Right then scales fell off Saul's eyes and he could see. We baptized him in the name of Jesus. As he ate his first food in three days, he told me how on the road, a bright light from heaven had flashed and knocked him down. A voice asked, "Saul, Saul, why do you persecute me?" The voice identified itself as Jesus.

From that moment Saul could not see. His companions led him to the house where Jesus had commanded him to go. Then Jesus commanded me to go to the same house to heal Saul.

Do you see how ★ *Jesus shows us the right path?*

Now Saul feels called to carry the good news about Jesus far and wide. I believe he will accomplish his goals by the grace of God and the power of the Holy Spirit!

I must leave you now, but I hope that someday we might meet again—in heaven if not before. Grace and peace to you, my young brothers and sisters!

Exit.

Published in *All Together Now, Volume 3* by Group Publishing, Inc., 1515 Cascade Ave., Loveland, CO 80538.

121

LIFE APPLICATION

Path Through the Bible

Say: ★*Jesus shows us the right path*, and we can trace that path all the way back through the Bible. We're going to make a little fold-out book that'll help you trace that path and remind you of it whenever you're wondering about which path to take in life.

Lead kids to your craft area where you've set out scissors, glue sticks, and copies of the "Pathway Through the Bible" handout (p. 123).

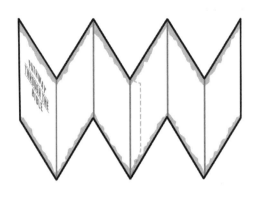

Help kids through the following steps to complete the handout.

✔ Cut out the two long sections.

✔ Make one long strip by gluing the tab at the end of the first section to the back of the second section.

✔ Accordion fold the pages to form a book.

When kids have their books assembled, say: **We have here five verses from throughout the Bible, starting toward the beginning and finishing with the words of Jesus, and they're all talking about the same path. The challenge for you is to read them and discover what path they're talking about.**

Select child volunteers to read the five Bible verses. Help them discover together that God's path, Jesus' path, is one of love.

COMMITMENT

Pathfinders

Say: **Let's talk for a moment about the times you're not sure which path to choose.**

Ask:

• What paths can you choose from when kids are making fun of another child?

Hold up a finished "Pathway Through the Bible" book.

Ask:

• Which verse in here might help you choose the right path?

Encourage kids to brainstorm other times they might choose between loving and unloving paths, such as when a parent asks for

All Together Now

PATHWAY THROUGH THE BIBLE

Understand, therefore, that the Lord your God is indeed God. He is the faithful God who keeps his covenant for a thousand generations and lavishes his unfailing love on those who love him and obey his commands.

Deuteronomy 7:9

How precious is your unfailing love, O God! All humanity finds shelter in the shadow of your wings.

Psalm 36:7

So the Lord must wait for you to come to him so he can show you his love and compassion. For the Lord is a faithful God. Blessed are those who wait for his help.

Isaiah 30:18

For the Lord your God is living among you. He is a mighty savior. He will take delight in you with gladness. With his love, he will calm all your fears. He will rejoice over you with joyful songs.

Zephaniah 3:17

Jesus replied, "The most important commandment is this: 'Listen, O Israel! The Lord our God is the one and only Lord. And you must love the Lord your God with all your heart, all your soul, all your mind, and all your strength.' The second is equally important: 'Love your neighbor as yourself.' "

Mark 12:29-31

(Glue next panel here)

123

help on a task that they really don't want to do or when a younger sibling is being annoying. Ask them to point out verses from their handouts that would help them choose the right path.

Say: ★ *Jesus shows us the right path.* **You can use your "Pathway Through the Bible" book to help you find those right choices. Here's a big hint: The right path will always be the path that shows God's love.**

CLOSING
....

Pathfinders Prayer

Gather kids for a closing prayer.

Pray: ★ *Jesus, thank you for showing us the right path.* **Thank you that the Bible is full of examples that you are loving and kind and that the right path always shows your love. Help us be careful pathfinders this week and look to you to help us make loving decisions. We pray in your name, amen.**

All Together Now

Saul Over the Wall

LESSON AIM

To help kids realize that ★ *Jesus makes us new inside.*

OBJECTIVES

Kids will

✓ paint pudding faces on themselves while hidden inside brown paper bags,

✓ experience Saul's transformational activities,

✓ make a Möbius craft strip that changes from the inside out, and

✓ pray for Jesus to make them new from the inside out.

BIBLE BASIS

 Acts 9:19-25

These things we can put together from Luke's writing about Saul: he was a man of tremendous intellectual and dialectical prowess and boundless energy, demanding, passionate, and self-sacrificing. Before he knew Jesus, we might label Saul a "type A" personality, a force of nature.

Have you ever known a "force of nature" person? Does it burn all your energy to be around an individual like that, or do you light up in the presence of such an inspiring individual? Your answer will depend in part on where you fall on personality charts. I like to observe from the back of the room

You'll need...

☐ selection of instant puddings*

☐ milk*

☐ small paper plates

☐ spoons

☐ large paper grocery bags

☐ smocks

☐ hair bands

☐ whistle

☐ paper towels

☐ mirror

☐ bowl of warm water

☐ Hula-Hoop

☐ 2 swimming noodles

☐ heavy woven laundry basket

☐ crayons

☐ scissors

☐ glue sticks

☐ tape

☐ copies of "The Marvelous Möbius" handout (p. 132)

☐ optional: digital or phone camera

* Always check for allergies before serving snacks.

and think through what the "force of nature" person has to say before I embrace his or her ideas.

But that's not all that's going on in this passage. Take this "force of nature" person and turn him in his tracks with a vision from Jesus laying open his sins against the church. Then watch as a kind, trusting Christian friend lays hands on him so he can receive the Holy Spirit of God. And now what does our "force of nature" person become? *A world changer!* Suddenly we see a turning point in early Christianity!

Had I been in Damascus at the time and had somehow been able to grasp the immensity of what God was doing, I would have hoisted a banner saying, "Watch out world—here comes Saul!" But I wouldn't have meant Saul alone, of course. I would have meant Saul completely transformed by the Holy Spirit, put to work for the kingdom of God at the perfect moment in history.

The Saul who was expected to show up in Damascus hunting Jesus-followers suddenly shows up preaching that Jesus is the Son of God. And doing it so effectively that no one can go against his arguments as, day by day, the Spirit is opening to him the relevance of Old Testament prophecies and how they apply to his newfound Savior. *This is Saul of Tarsus?* cry the Jews in dismay. *We thought he was on our side!*

The Jews could barely take in the retrofitting of Saul by God. The Christians could only rejoice to call him one of their own. Saul had grown up in Tarsus, an ancient city known for its schools and philosophical circles. He had probably traveled to Jerusalem as a young child to receive his formal religious training, some of which took place under Gamaliel, the greatest teacher of that generation. His conversion took place in Damascus, a city that rivaled Tarsus in its ancient beginnings and long-admired intellectual tradition.

To pull all these pieces together, God had crafted the best human vessel to carry Christianity to the Hellenistic world, to speak persuasively to learned ones at the Acropolis in Athens of their unknown God, to persuade kings and indeed to pierce Rome itself with the news of a self-sacrificing Savior who sits at the right hand of God Almighty.

So powerful was his teaching that the very men who sent him had no recourse but to order his death. He wasn't one who could be casually brushed aside with a fly swatter. Death was the only way to silence his dynamic witness. So Saul's Christian buddies lowered him in a basket (reminding us of Moses and the spies whom Rahab helped) over the city wall, and he survived his first scrape with death.

All Together Now

📖 **Psalm 107**

Many children used to memorize verse 2 of this Psalm as "Let the redeemed of the Lord say so."

Saul wasted no time doing that.

In his commentary on Acts, pastor and author Lloyd J. Ogilvie observes the importance of new Christians verbalizing their stories to cement their new faith and to give encouragement to others. It's truly difficult to imagine the effect on the believers at Damascus when God transformed Saul from dreaded enemy to staunch ally.

Imagine the fear Saul stirred in the hearts of the anti-Christian Jews. They knew immediately what they faced in Saul as an enemy.

UNDERSTANDING YOUR KIDS

Before his conversion, Saul was, in a very real way, a bully. Children know a lot about bullies. Scholastic.com states that 20 to 30 percent of school-age children are involved in bullying incidents. Think about the kids in your group. Which of them might be easy targets for bullies? Which might be bullies themselves?

I've long wondered if kids' fascination with superheroes comes from the desire to have such a being on their side in the world of reality. In today's Bible passage we see that through God's astounding transformation of Saul, Saul changes roles from bully to Holy Spirit-powered superhero of the early church.

Use this lesson to help kids discover that only God can make us new inside to the extent that Saul was instantly transformed. Help them see that any individual, no matter how threatening, is a candidate for God's ultimate transforming power.

THE LESSON »

ATTENTION GRABBER

Pudding Faces

Greet kids warmly as they arrive and tell them that you're going to let them become someone they've never been before.

Have kids gather around the table and uncover the puddings, spoons, paper plates, paper grocery bags, and smocks. Have everyone don smocks.

Say: **In just a few moments I'm going to let you go undercover—under the cover of your grocery bags. But first, you'll need to dab *small amounts* of pudding onto your plates. The pudding is not to eat, but to change your appearance. You can dip up different colors with your fingers to paint your face, nose, or cheeks as you like. The key is to use just little bits, not big globs. Everybody repeat: *Little bits, not big globs.***

Pause for kids to repeat.

Say: **You can do anything you like except make a big mess! To add to the fun, you're not going to know exactly what you'll look like, because you'll be pudding-painting yourselves inside your brown paper bags. For those of you with longer hair, I'll help you tie back your hair.**

Have kids line up to gather their pudding palettes. Make sure kids take fairly small amounts of each flavor of pudding. As they stand around, help them put the paper sacks over their heads. For the easiest cleanup later, hand out paper towels at this time. Then blow your whistle to begin the pudding-painting session.

As you see the majority of kids running low on pudding, blow your whistle again to bring the painting to a stop. Instruct kids to wipe their hands with paper towels, but keep their paper bags on. Give a three-two-one countdown for the big reveal. Have kids enjoy each others' looks before you break out a mirror so kids can see themselves. If possible, take a group photo of your pudding-faced kids. Have them leave their yummy faces on as you circle up for discussion.

Ask:

• **What is it like to see your friends painted in silly pudding faces?**

• **What did you think when you finally saw your own face?**

• **How does having decorated faces change who you are on the inside?**

Say: **Today we're going to learn that only ★ *Jesus makes***

Prep Box

Prepare instant pudding in a few colorful flavors such as chocolate, pistachio, banana cream, and cheesecake. Set out a spoon, a small paper plate, a large paper grocery bag, and a smock for each child. Cover the table with the bags and smocks to surprise the kids.

Teacher Tip

The key to keeping this activity neat and manageable in the meeting area is to have kids use *small* amounts of pudding for spots and streaks, not large globs for covering whole areas of the face.

All Together Now

us new inside. **And when he changes us, he does it in a** *big way.*

Now how about cleaning yourselves up in a big way by finding a partner, dipping your paper towels into warm water, and wiping all that yummy stuff off your faces and hands!

BIBLE EXPLORATION

....

Saul Over the Wall (Acts 9:19-25)

Say: **Line up facing me, because you're each going to have a turn being Saul.**

Have a helper at ready with a Hula-Hoop, swimming noodles, and laundry basket.

Say: **Saul had been a big bully to Christians. But when he met Jesus on the road to Damascus,** ★*Jesus made him new inside.*

Have your helper with the Hula-Hoop frame each child in turn. First, have the children show their meanest bully face. Then have them spin around and show a nice-guy face.

Say: **Once Jesus had made Saul new on the inside, Saul couldn't wait to go to the synagogue and tell everyone there that Jesus is Lord.**

To represent the Jewish synagogue, have an assistant help hold two swimming noodles over the head of each child in turn. Have the children "preach": "Jesus is Lord!"

Say: **Day after day Saul went to the synagogues in Damascus and preached. Filled with the Holy Spirit, he was a powerful preacher. No one could argue with him!**

Have your assistant frame each child in turn with the Hula-Hoop. As the kids are framed, have them show their "powerful" muscles.

Say: **The Jews in the synagogues were confused. "Isn't this the Saul who was supposed to come and get rid of the Christians?" they asked.**

Have your assistant frame each child in turn with the Hula-Hoop. As the kids are framed, have them scratch their heads in confusion.

Say: **The Jews knew they had to do something to stop Saul's powerful preaching for Jesus. They thought about beating him up, but knew he'd be right back preaching the next day.**

> ## Teacher Tip
>
> If you have a faucet or rest-room nearby, you may want to send kids there for cleanup. But a simple in-room cleanup will save valuable minutes for your lesson.

Have your assistant hand the swimming noodles to each child in turn. Have the children beat the noodles together, as if they were beating Saul.

Say: **Finally the synagogue leaders decided there was only one thing to do. They would have to kill Saul to keep him quiet!**

Have your assistant frame each child in turn with the Hula-Hoop. As the kids are framed, have them cover their mouths with both hands.

Say: **Their plan was to plant spies at the city gate to see when Saul left. Then they would get him!**

Have your assistant frame each child with the swimming noodles to represent the city gate. Have the children walk in place on tiptoes and dart their eyes to the left and right, pretending to be spies.

Say: **But Saul had friends everywhere, and they got word of this terrible plan.**

Have your assistant cup a hand over the ear of each child in turn and pretend to whisper. Have the children listen carefully and then nod as if they understand the plan to kill Saul.

Say: **So Saul's Christian friends came up with a plan to save Saul's life. And it was a clever plan!**

Have your assistant hand the basket to each child in turn. Have the children look into the basket and then wink and hand it back to the assistant.

Say: **They waited until night fell. Then they had Saul sit in a basket and they lowered it with ropes over the city wall.**

Have your assistant set the basket on a low table. If possible, one by one, have the children sit in the basket as you and your assistant lower it to the floor.

Say: **And that's how Saul lived to preach another day! Wherever he went he preached the gospel of Jesus, because ★ *Jesus had made him new inside!***

Lead kids in a round of applause for their part in telling the Bible passage. Then gather them in a discussion circle.

Ask:

• **What made such a huge difference in Saul that he changed from a bully of Christians to a great preacher for Jesus?**

• **How was the "new" Saul different from the "old" Saul?**

• **What does it feel like when ★ *Jesus makes us new inside*?**

All Together Now

• **What's one way Jesus has helped you be fresh and new on the inside?**

If one or more children seems ready to put their faith in Jesus, plan to speak with them afterward.

LIFE APPLICATION
•••
The Marvelous Möbius

Say: **Only ★ *Jesus makes us new inside*. Only Jesus can cause the huge change that Saul experienced. Saul wasn't just putting on an act or pretending to be different—God truly made him brand-new from the inside out. The people who knew him hardly knew what to think about this new Saul!**

I have a fun craft called a Möbius strip that demonstrates what it's like to be new from the inside out.

Lead kids to your craft table where you've set out crayons (not markers which would bleed through), scissors, glue sticks, tape, and copies of "The Marvelous Möbius" handout (p. 132). Lead kids through the following steps to complete their handouts.

✓ On the blank side of the handout, have kids color a bright, bold pattern over the rectangle from which the Möbius will be formed. It's fine to color outside the lines.

✓ Have them flip the paper to the front side and decorate the front of the rectangle in a different pattern and colors.

✓ Have them cut the three strips of the Möbius apart and glue them end to end. It's fine to reinforce the glued ends with tape.

✓ Making one twist, pull the end of the strip around and glue and tape it to the beginning, forming a circle. Now kids have a circle with a twist that has no end—called a Möbius strip.

Say: **Jesus took Saul and, starting on the inside, made him a completely new person. When you examine your Möbius strips, you'll find that's exactly what happens to them. They start out as one pattern and then turn into another. Jesus provides that turning point when we believe in him!**

The Marvelous Möbius

Turn the paper to the blank side and color a beautiful design on the back of the rectangle that will form the Möbius. It's fine if you go outside the lines. Then turn the paper to the printed side and decorate it. Next, cut out the rectangle and cut apart the three strips. Glue one strip to the next to make one long strip. Make one twist and join the first strip to the last to form a marvelous Möbius circle!

Jesus makes us new inside!

Jesus makes us new inside!

GLUE

Jesus makes us new inside!

Jesus makes us new inside!

GLUE

Jesus makes us new inside!

Jesus makes us new inside!

GLUE

COMMITMENT

....

Inside-Out Change

Have kids bring their complete "Marvelous Möbius" projects and join you in a circle. Encourage kids to show each other how different their Möbius projects look on the inside and the outside.

This is the perfect time to ask kids about their experiences with Jesus.

Ask:

• Describe a time when you saw others talk about their faith in Jesus.

• How do you feel about sharing your faith in Jesus with others?

• What's the difference between saying we love Jesus and showing that we love him?

CLOSING

....

New Inside

Have kids loop their "Marvelous Möbius" projects over their wrists and then pile their hands together in the center of a circle.

Pray: **God, we believe that your Son ★ *Jesus makes us new inside.* We know that if he can change a man like Saul, he can surely change us. God, help us look to you every day so we can reflect the newness of life that only you can give us. Help us not try to be cool or popular, but to be like Jesus instead. Thank you for making us new from the inside out. In Jesus' name, amen.**

Safe in a Shipwreck

LESSON AIM

To help kids realize that ★ *we can trust God all the time.*

OBJECTIVES

Kids will

✓ play a game of Made You Flinch,

✓ recreate Paul's shipwreck on the island of Malta,

✓ create a "Verses of Hope" box, and

✓ share how they'll share their Verses of Hope with others.

BIBLE BASIS

 Acts 27:1—28:10

With this passage we jump nearly to the end of the book of Acts. One way to focus on the ministry of Paul is to read about him in Acts in one fell swoop. Begin with Acts 7:54–8:3, read Acts 9, and then move to Acts 13 and read straight through to the end. It may take you half an hour. You'll be overwhelmed by the stunning impact one man had on the world when led and empowered by the Holy Spirit to take the message of Jesus far and wide in the Roman Empire, planting and tending churches and finally breaking free from those who would sub-ject Christians to strict adherence of Jewish law. The first part of Acts tells of the birth of the church; the second part, with Paul and friends, tells of its spread and establishment through-out the known world. Read the passage—catch the vision!

You'll need...

☐ table(s)

☐ blue crepe paper for streamers

☐ 2 spray bottles of water

☐ crackers*

☐ copies of the "Verses of Hope" handout (p. 142)

☐ scissors

* Always check for allergies before serving snacks.

In this account you'll note Saul's name changes to Paul. We see this for the first time in Acts 13:9. *Saul* was the apostle's Jewish name. He was from the tribe of Benjamin, the same tribe as King Saul. *Saul* means "asked [of God]." *Paul* was a name that would be more easily accepted in Greek and Roman society. Its meaning is "little" or "little guy." In this time period it was typical for Jews to use two names, one in Israelite society and the other in Hellenistic/Roman society.

After Paul has traveled along the Mediterranean coast, into the depths of Greece and modern-day Turkey, he determines to return to speak his truth in Jerusalem. Warned by many not to do so, he makes the journey anyway, only to be rescued from a riot by Roman soldiers. Paul's young nephew discovered a plot to kill the apostle, which he reported to the commander at Jerusalem. The commander had Paul transported by night under heavy guard to the Roman governor Felix at Caesarea. Felix let the case languish for two years until he was replaced by Festus. The Jews demanded that Paul be delivered to Jerusalem for trial. When Festus questioned Paul about his willingness to be tried in Jerusalem, Paul, claiming his right as a Roman citizen, appealed to Caesar.

So began a long journey to Rome. Placed in the care of the centurion Julius, Paul received deferential treatment. By the time they boarded a merchant vessel bound for Rome, it was too late in the season to make the sea crossing safely. The ship ended up in the throes of a terrible storm that tossed and battered the ship across the Adriatic Sea to the point that there seemed little hope of surviving.

However, an angel appeared to Paul and assured him that although the ship would indeed wreck, everyone on board would be saved. Paul passed this message on to all 276 souls aboard and encouraged them to eat.

And so they all arrived safely on the island of Malta according to Paul's prediction. Natives welcomed them with a bonfire. The Holy Spirit was with Paul and allowed him to perform miracles of healing as they wintered there.

📖 Psalm 65:7

In Hebrew literature, the sea, the depths, the abyss represent the fearful unknown. Think of God parting the Red Sea for the Hebrew people to walk through, and then drowning the armies of Pharaoh in its depths. Think of disobedient Jonah being cast into the sea, and then calling out, "I cried out to the Lord in my great trouble, and he answered me. I called to you from the land of the dead, and Lord, you heard me!" (Jonah 2:2). And again of the disciples worshipping Jesus after he calmed the storm at sea (Matthew 8:25-27).

For two weeks the people on Paul's ship had feared imminent death in the depths of the sea at the hand of an unrelenting storm. But, reassured by a vision from God, Paul became the voice of hope.

This psalm proclaims faith in God to overpower the raging ocean and pounding waves. I wonder if Paul had it in mind when he confidently took charge of seeing to it that everyone reached shore safely.

UNDERSTANDING YOUR KIDS

Every now and then the media grabs our attention with a story about a very young child who saves a parent's life by dialing 911 or by guiding a vehicle to the shoulder of the road and stopping it. Where does this unusual presence of mind come from? What is different in these children compared to those who can do little to improve the situation, but instead scream or cry hysterically?

Some would tell us that such presence of mind is a built-in personality trait. Others might argue that it's the result of careful training by parents. There may be some cultural mindset thrown in. Perhaps it's a combination of all three.

This we can say for sure: Those who have a deep and abiding faith in an omnipotent God can face the most terrifying situations with a different mindset than others. It takes training and personal experience with the living God to reach that point of faith.

Use this lesson to teach your kids that they are no less in God's hands in a frightening situation than they are sitting safely in a favorite chair at home. Because God is all-seeing and all-powerful, they can be calm and confident that God's purposes will be accomplished in their lives despite how things appear. And, like Paul, they can encourage others to embrace hope as well.

THE LESSON >>

ATTENTION GRABBER

Made You Flinch

Greet kids warmly and tell them there's great adventure ahead.

Say: **We're going to start off with a little game of Made You Flinch.** Explain to kids that they'll make a long line all the way across your meeting area, facing the center of the room. You'll walk up behind them and pop up here and there trying to surprise the kids and make them jump or flinch a little. The kids' job is *not* to flinch and to hold perfectly still. Tell kids they have to continue looking toward the center of the room.

Creep along behind the line of kids. Every now and then, jump out and shout "Boo!" or "Hi there!" causing kids to jump. You can also surprise them from behind with a bright "Hello!" in someone's ear. Increase your repertoire of surprising messages as your imagination guides you, but only speak, never touch.

When you've gotten a flinch out of most of the kids, announce that it's time to try your game a different way. Have your kids form two rows and pack themselves tightly together for mutual support.

Say: **Let's see how you do when you're arranged this way.**

Repeat your surprising little messages, jumping out at kids when they're not expecting it. Kids may still jump some, but chances are they'll flinch less as they feel support from the other members of the group. After you've had several tries at making kids flinch, gather everyone together in a discussion circle and ask:

• **How was the first game different from the second?**

• **Describe why you flinched more in the first game than the second.**

Say: **We never know when something in life is going to jump out at us and make us flinch. But the truth is, we're never alone when that happens because we serve an all-knowing, all-powerful God. And ★** *we can trust God all the time.* **That helps us stay calm and confident even when other people around us feel afraid. That's exactly what happens with the hero of today's Bible passage. The circumstances are scarier than you can imagine. But our hero trusts in God. Just wait and see what happens!**

All Together Now

BIBLE EXPLORATION

Safe in a Shipwreck (Acts 27:1–28:10)

Say: **We begin today's passage on board a ship. Let's create a ship by turning a table upside down.**

Okay, passengers, board the ship!

Now, let me tell you a little about your ship. It started from Egypt filled with wheat, bound for Rome. Find things around the room you can load into the ship to represent cargo.

Pause as kids load books and other items they can find in the room to represent cargo into their ship.

Say: **One of the passengers is someone you might be familiar with—the Apostle Paul. We've called him Saul before, but he also goes by the name Paul. I need a volunteer to be Paul.**

Choose a child volunteer. Have him or her stand and then sit down again.

Say: **What I didn't mention is that Paul was a prisoner on his way to Rome to have his case heard by Caesar. Paul was arrested by Jews in Jerusalem for teaching about Jesus. He'd been in prison for a long time waiting for his case to be heard. Finally he appealed his case to Caesar. That meant he had to travel all the way to Rome, across the sea.**

Here was the problem: It was only safe to cross the sea during certain seasons. Once winter arrived, dangerous storms made sea crossings far too risky, so most ships waited until spring. But the captain of this ship decided to sail anyway.

Who wants to be our captain?

We also need Paul's special guard, a centurion named Julius.

Have a Julius volunteer sit next to Paul.

Say: **Paul talked to the ship's captain and told him there'd be trouble if they tried to sail this late in the season.**

Have Paul and the Captain stand and appear to discuss the issue.

Say: **But the captain decided to sail anyway. They weren't at sea very long before they got caught in a great storm. Waves and wind tossed the ship along.**

Toss strips of crepe paper streamers to the kids.

Say: **Use these to make huge waves that wash over the ship.**

> ### Teacher Tip
> Depending on the size of the table and the number of children in your group, you may need to turn two tables upside down to create your ship. Place the tables side by side.

> ### Teacher Tip
> It's fine to use a female volunteer for a male role.

Squirt water from spray bottles into the air to make the storm more fierce.

Say: **Lean all the way to the left as the ship tips that way. Now lean all the way to the right as the ship tips that way.**

The sailors threw all the cargo overboard, hoping to keep the ship from breaking apart.

Pause for the kids to throw out their cargo.

Say: **People were too scared to eat or drink. Almost two weeks passed this way, with no sign of the sun or a break in the storm.**

Then one morning Paul stood and encouraged the people.

Pause for Paul to stand and mimic speaking.

Say: **He said, "You've been so worried that you haven't touched food in almost two weeks. Please eat something now for your own good, for everyone will make it off this ship alive."**

The people on the ship believed Paul and had a little to eat.

Give each of the kids a cracker and invite them to eat.

Say: **Soon the sailors realized they were near land. They lowered the anchors at the back of the ship so they would be slowly pulled toward land, but the ship got grounded on a sandbar before it got all the way to shore.**

The captain gave orders for those who could swim to jump overboard and swim to shore. Everyone else hung on to a piece of the ship as it broke apart and rode it into shore. Just as Paul promised, everyone made it to shore safely!

Have kids jump overboard and "swim" to a certain wall, which is the "shore."

Paul never doubted that he and everyone else on the ship were in God's hands. He gave a message of hope and encouragement at just the right time. Paul knew that ★ *we can trust God all the time*. Now you know it too!

Gather kids in a discussion circle and ask:

• **Describe how you react when a big storm comes. What scares you most?**

• **Describe what helps you feel better during a big storm.**

• **In scary situations, how can we remember that ★ *we can trust God all the time?***

All Together Now

LIFE APPLICATION

Verses of Hope

Say: **The Bible is full of verses of hope that remind us that ★** *we can trust God all the time.* **Today you can make your very own cool little box of some of those verses!**

Lead kids to a table where you've set out scissors and copies of the "Verses of Hope" handout (p. 142). Show kids the sample you've made.

Say: **This craft is very simple. Cut out the box and the strip of Bible verses. Write your name somewhere on the box. Keep folding the box piece on the dotted lines until it folds in and forms a box. Then fold up the verse strip so it fits inside the box. Slip the tab on the box into the slit and your box is securely closed!**

Prep Box

Make a sample of the Verses of Hope box and the folded verses that go inside. Also, slit the handouts on the straight line on the box so kids will be able to close their boxes.

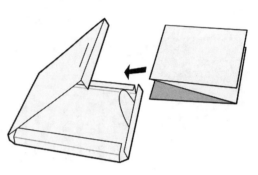

COMMITMENT

Hope in a Box

Gather kids in a circle with their completed handouts.

Say: **Do you know what you have here? You have hope in a box! That's right! Not everybody has hope in a box, you know.**

Ask:

• **Describe whether you think hope is something you keep all to yourself or you share it—and why.**

• **Tell about a situation when you shared hope with someone else.**

• **Why do you think knowing Jesus stops us from running out of hope?**

Say: **There's nothing better than knowing ★** *we can trust God all the time.* **Turn to a friend and think of a time that you can share your hope verses this week.**

Verses of Hope

Paul helped all the people aboard the sinking ship when he told them everyone would make it to shore alive. Use these verses of hope to "steady your ship" when scary things come your way!

Lord, you know the hopes of the helpless. Surely you will hear their cries and comfort them.
Psalm 10:17

But the Lord watches over those who fear him, those who rely on his unfailing love.
Psalm 33:18

The name of the Lord is a strong fortress; the godly run to him and are safe.
Proverbs 18:10

Do not be afraid, for I have ransomed you. I have called you by name; you are mine.
Isaiah 43:1

And we know that God causes everything to work together for the good of those who love God and are called according to his purpose for them.
Romans 8:28

Give all your worries and cares to God, for he cares about you.
1 Peter 5:7

CLOSING

. . . .

Trust Prayer

Say: **Today we learned that ★** *we can trust God all the time.*

Ask:

• **What are scary times you might face when you'll need to trust God?**

• **How did Paul encourage others in the shipwreck?**

• **How can you remember to be like Paul the next time you face something scary?**

Gather kids in a tight circle.

Say: **When we believe in Jesus and have the Holy Spirit in our lives, God can help us do anything, anything at all. Read these power verses every day, and you'll grow in your trust of God's love and power for you. Let's pray now for that trust. I invite you to share one way you can trust God with something in your life.**

Invite kids to describe one way they'll trust God. Speak first, with your own way to trust God, such as, "God, I trust you to provide for my family's needs." When kids who want to share have, say:

God, we trust in your love and power. Help us to embrace you in faith. In Jesus' name, amen.

Now, go in the power of the Holy Spirit, believing that ★ *we can trust God all the time!*